SPECTR

WORKBOOK 4

A Communicative Course in English

David P. Rein
with Donald R. H. Byrd

Donald R. H. Byrd *Project Director*

Prentice Hall Regents
Englewood Cliffs, NJ   07632

Project Manager: Nancy L. Leonhardt
Manager of Development Services: Louisa B. Hellegers
Development Editor: Tünde A. Dewey
Production Editor: Paula D. Williams
Contributing Writer: Karen Davy

Director of Production and Manufacturing: David Riccardi
Editorial Production/Design Manager: Dominick Mosco
Electronic Production Coordinator: Molly Pike-Riccardi
Technical Support and Assistance: Freddie Flake, Todd Ware
Production Coordinator: Ray Keating

Cover Design: Roberto de Vicq
Interior Design: Anna Veltfort
Audio Editor: Andrew Gitzy
Audio Program Producer: Paul Ruben Productions

ACKNOWLEDGMENTS

Illustrations: pp. 10, 21, 36, 47, 52, 62 (top), 63, 67, 74, 81, 91, 99, 104, 108, 117, 119 by Arnie Ten; pp. 1, 3, 9, 17, 25, 28, 35, 43, 51, 60, 61, 64, 69, 71, 77, 85, 86, 93, 95, 103, 107, 111, 114 by Gene Myers; pp. 37, 53 by Anna Veltfort; pp 2, 12, 27, 38, 44, 56, 62 (bottom), 65, 72, 80, 89, 100, 105, 106, 112, 116 by Anne Burgess; p. 96, by Bot Roda; pp. 45, 48, 58 by Sylvio Redinger; pp. 6 (puzzle), 13 (journal), 16, 19, 20 (ads), p. 24 (movie ad), 31, 32 (invitation), 33, 66, 68, 70, 76, 79, 84, 88, 92, 97, 98, 102, 110 by Don Martinetti.

Photos: p. 5, Charlie Chaplin, p. 8 Colonial Williamsburg, Colonial Williamsburg p. 18-1 The Taj Mahal, United Nations, p. 18-2 Christopher Columbus, Metropolitan Museum of Art, p. 18-3 Thomas Edison, AP/Wide World Photos

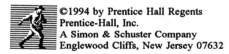

©1994 by Prentice Hall Regents
Prentice-Hall, Inc.
A Simon & Schuster Company
Englewood Cliffs, New Jersey 07632

Printed in the United States of America
10 9 8

ISBN   0-13-830167-0

Prentice Hall International (UK) Limited, *London*
Prentice Hall of Australia Pty. Limited, *Sydney*
Prentice Hall Canada, Inc., *Toronto*
Prentice Hall Hispanoamericana, S.A., *Mexico*
Prentice Hall of India Private Limited, *New Delhi*
Prentice Hall of Japan, Inc., *Tokyo*
Simon & Schuster Asia Pte. Ltd, *Singapore*
Editora Prentice Hall do Brasil, Ltda., *Rio de Janeiro*

INTRODUCTION

Spectrum 4 represent the fourth level of a six-level course designed for adolescent and adult learners of English. The student books, workbooks, and audio cassette programs for each level provide practice in all four communication skills, with a special focus on listening and speaking. The first four levels are offered in split editions—1A, 1B, 2A, 2B, 3A, 3B, 4A, and 4B. The student books, workbooks, teacher's editions, and audio programs for levels 1 to 4 are also available in full editions.

Spectrum is a "communicative" course in English, based on the idea that communication is not merely an end-product of language study, but rather the very process through which a new language is acquired. Since the starting point for communication is understanding, the student books, workbooks, and audio program emphasize the importance of comprehension, both as a useful skill and as a natural means of acquiring a language. *Spectrum* considers interaction to be another vital step in language acquisition. Student books offer both focused and open-ended interactive practice. Workbooks offer written practice of new functions and structures and guided composition activities preparing students for written interaction.

Workbook 4 is closely coordinated with **Student Book 4**. Both consist of seven units divided into one- and two-page lessons. Review lessons follow Units 1 to 4 and Units 5 to 7. The workbook provides listening and writing practice to reinforce material introduced in the corresponding student book lesson:

- After students listen to and read the opening conversations in the student book unit, they write down similar conversations as they complete matching, sequencing, fill-in, and multiple-choice activities.

- For each thematic lesson in the student book, students complete workbook exercises offering additional writing practice on new functions and structures.

- The one-page comprehension lesson in the student book leads to a variety of listening activities in the workbook designed to focus students' attention on functions, structures, and aspects of pronunciation. All listening activities are recorded on cassette.

- After reading a realistic document in the final lesson of the student book unit, students have the opportunity to write down personal thoughts and information as they complete a related composition activity.

Audio Cassette Program 4 offers two cassettes for the student book and one cassette for the workbook. All listening activities are dramatized by professional actors in realistic recordings with sound effects.

In addition to step-by-step instructions for the student book, **Teacher's Edition 4** contains listening scripts and answer keys for the workbook.

REVIEWERS AND CONSULTANTS

Prentice Hall Regents would like to thank the following long-time users of *Spectrum*, whose insights and suggestions have helped to shape the content and format of the new edition: Motofumi Aramaki, *Sony Language Laboratory*, Tokyo, Japan; *Associacão Cultural Brasil-Estados Unidos (ACBEU)*, Salvador-Bahia, Brazil; *AUA Language Center*, Bangkok, Thailand, Thomas J. Kral and faculty; Pedro I. Cohen, Professor Emeritus of English, Linguistics, and Education, *Universidad de Panamá*; *ELSI Taiwan Language Schools*, Taipei, Taiwan, Kenneth Hou and faculty; James Hale, *Sundai ELS*, Tokyo, Japan; *Impact*, Santiago, Chile; *Instituto Brasil-Estados Unidos (IBEU)*, Rio de Janeiro, Brazil; *Instituto Brasil-Estados Unidos No Ceará (IBEU-CE)*, Fortaleza, Brazil; *Instituto Chileno Norteamericano de Cultura*, Santiago, Chile; *Instituto Cultural Argentino Norteamericano (ICANA)*, Buenos Aires, Argentina; Christopher M. Knott, *Chris English Masters Schools*, Kyoto, Japan; *The Language Training and Testing Center*, Taipei, Taiwan, Anthony Y. T. Wu and faculty; *Lutheran Language Institute*, Tokyo, Japan; *Network Cultura, Ensino e Livraria Ltda*, São Paulo, Brazil; *Seven Language and Culture*, São Paulo, Brazil.

SPECIAL ACKNOWLEDGMENTS FOR LEVEL 4

Blanca Arazi, Instituto Cultural Argentino Norteamericano (ICANA), Buenos Aires, Argentina; Instituto Chileno Norteamericano de Cultura, Santiago, Chile; Peter Herzog, ELS Language Center, St. Paul, MN; Kevin McClure, ELS Language Center, San Francisco, CA; William McCormack, AUA Language Center, Bangkok, Thailand; Margaret Pennings, ELS Language Center, St. Paul, MN.

CONTENTS

CONTENTS

Lesson 1

▶ **Complete the conversations with the sentences in the box.**

You did? How was it?   Nothing much. What's new with you?
Hi, Connie! How are you?   That's great!
Did you read any good books over the summer?   To tell you the truth, I didn't think it was *that* interesting.
Did you do anything special over the summer?   No, but I've always wanted to go.
You aren't?   I've read it, too. It's interesting, isn't it?
Oh, I've read Sheldon's latest book.

1. **A** *Hi, Connie! How are you?* _____

   B Just fine, thanks. What's new?

   A _____

   B Well, I'm not working at the video store anymore.

   A _____

   B No. I've decided to go back to school.

   A _____

2. **A** _____

   B We visited Robert's family in southern France.

   A _____

   B Wonderful! It was one of the nicest vacations we've ever

   taken. You've never been to France, have you?

   A _____

3. **A** _____

   B As a matter of fact, I read a couple of novels by Sidney Sheldon.

   A _____

   B You have?

   C _____

   B It really is.

   A _____

Lesson 2

1 ► Listen to each conversation. Does the speaker have a good opinion or a bad opinion? Check (✔) the correct column.

	GOOD	BAD		GOOD	BAD
1.	✔	____	4.	____	____
2.	____	____	5.	____	____
3.	____	____	6.	____	____

2 ► Complete the conversation with appropriate words.

A ___*Did*___ you do _____ special _____ the summer?

B We _____ a trip _____ Europe.

A _____, really? _____ was it?

B Terrible! _____ was one _____ the worst vacations we've _____ taken.

3 ► Complete the questions in the Trivia Quiz with the superlative form of the adjectives in parentheses. Then try to answer the questions before you look at the answers at the bottom of the page. (Note that all the questions are about the United States.)

U.S. TRIVIA QUIZ

1. What is _the most popu-_ _____ (popular) flavor of ice cream? _Vanilla_

2. What is _____ (common) last name? _____

3. How old was _____ (old) man when he died? _____

4. How tall was _____ (tall) man? _____

5. Where is _____ (low) and _____ (hot) place? _____

6. What is _____ (dry) state? _____

7. In what state would you find _____ (cloudy) place? _____ And _____ (snowy)? _____

8. What is _____ (small) state? _____ And _____ (large)? _____

Answers:
1. Vanilla
2. Smith
3. 137
4. 8′ X 11″
5. California (Death Valley)
6. Nevada
7. Oregon, Washington
8. Rhode Island, Alaska

2 Unit 1

4 ► **Rick Estrada, a TV sportscaster, spoke to some fans after a soccer game. Write Rick's questions, asking for opinions in as many ways as you can. Then write appropriate answers, using the superlative form of the adjectives and the present perfect form of the verbs in parentheses.**

Rick *What did you think of the game?*

Jack (interesting, see) *It was one of the most interesting games I've ever seen.*

Rick _____

Lori (disappointing, be to) _____

_____

Rick _____

Eric (exciting, go to) _____

_____

Rick _____

Dave (good, attend) _____

_____

Rick _____

Kate (bad, see) _____

_____

5 ► **Answer the questions with your own information.**

1. What are the best and the worst movies you've ever seen?

_____

2. What is the most expensive thing you've ever bought?

_____

3. Who is the most interesting person you've ever met? Describe him or her.

_____

_____

4. What was the most enjoyable day you've ever had? Describe it.

_____

_____

Lesson 3

1 ▶ **Complete the conversation with rejoinders showing surprise.**

A Hi, Molly! What's new?

B Well, I'm getting married next Saturday.

A *You are?*

B Yes, and I'm so excited!

A Who are you marrying?

B I don't think you know him. He's from Sweden.

A _____

B Uh-huh. He used to be a professional tennis player.

A _____

B Yes, and he was a good one.

A _____

B Well, that's what he told me. We've only known each other for six months.

A _____ That's not very long.

B I know, but we fell in love at first sight.

A _____ Hmm … I don't believe in love at first sight.

B _____ Well, maybe it will happen to you someday.

2 ▶ **Listen to each statement and react to it, choosing from the rejoinders in the box.**

You can't?	I shouldn't?
They did?	She has?
He didn't?	He can?
They're not?	You won't?
You don't?	It is?
They have?	You aren't?

1. *He can?* _____
2. _____
3. _____
4. _____
5. _____
6. _____

7. _____
8. _____
9. _____
10. _____
11. _____
12. _____

3 ▶ **Write statements for these reactions. Use your own information.**

1. **A** *I'm going to take a trip to Antarctica next year.*
   B You are?
2. **A** _____
   B You have?
3. **A** _____
   B You didn't?
4. **A** _____
   B You can?

4 Unit 1

Lesson 4

1 ▶ **Find four conversations, using the sentences in the box.**

> Charlie Chaplin wasn't very funny, was he?
> To tell you the truth, I don't think he was *that* funny.
> Charlie Chaplin's movies are really funny, aren't they?
> No, they really aren't.
> Actually, I think he was *very* funny.
> Charlie Chaplin was really funny, wasn't he?
> Yes, they really are.
> Charlie Chaplin's movies aren't very funny, are they?

1. **A** *Charlie Chaplin's movies are really funny, aren't they?*

   B *Yes, they really are.*

2. **A** _____

   B _____

3. **A** _____

   B _____

4. **A** _____

   B _____

2 ▶ **Complete the conversations with tag questions.**

1. **A** You graduated from Jefferson High School, _____*didn't you?*_____

   B Yes. And you were in my class, _____

   A Your name is Sarah, _____ But you don't remember my name,

   _____

2. **A** The weather's been awful lately, _____

   B Yeah, it hasn't stopped raining for days, _____

   A Well, at least the grass won't be brown anymore, _____

   B That's true. In fact, it's going to be very green, _____

Lesson 5

① ▸ **English speakers often leave out certain words when they talk. Rewrite the underlined sentences, adding the words that are missing.**

1. <u>Still raining?</u>
   Is it still raining?

2. <u>Sounds like fun.</u>

   _____

3. <u>Anything interesting happen to you today?</u>

   _____

4. <u>Got to go. See you later.</u>

   _____

5. <u>Ever been to Williamsburg?</u>

   _____

6. <u>Got any stamps?</u>

   _____

7. I have an appointment with Mr. Collins. <u>You too?</u>

   _____

8. <u>Sorry I'm late. Got caught in traffic.</u>

   _____

② ▸ **Complete the crossword puzzle.**

Across

1. Surprising, in a negative way
5. Not very expensive
7. Soccer is one _____ the most popular sports in the world.
10. Like a child
11. Without dirt
12. Helpful
15. The superlative of *good*
16. The opposite of *ancient*
18. The opposite of *boring*
21. New Year's Day is a _____ in the U.S.
22. Not interesting

Down

2. "You are" is a rejoinder showing _____.
3. The opposite of *easy*
4. Very interesting
6. Costing a lot of money
8. The opposite of 11 across
9. The opposite of 6 down
13. I don't work _____ the bank anymore.
14. The opposite of 15 across
17. The season that follows winter
19. Not hard
20. Close

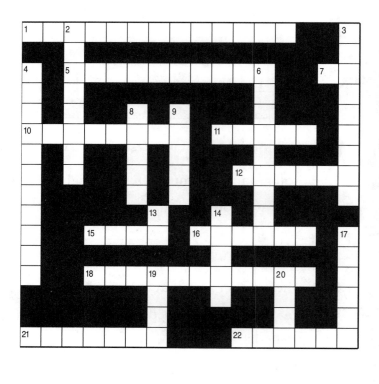

Lesson 6

 1 ▶ Listen to each conversation. Is the first speaker asking for information or giving an opinion and asking if the second speaker agrees? Check (✔) the correct column.

	INFORMATION	OPINION
1.	_____	__✔__
2.	_____	_____
3.	_____	_____
4.	_____	_____
5.	_____	_____
6.	_____	_____

 2 ▶ Listen and agree with the speakers. Write short answers.

1. *Yes, it is,* _____

2. _____

3. _____

4. _____

5. _____

6. _____

7. _____

8. _____

3 ▶ Listen to the conversations. The first sentence in each conversation ends with a tag question. Mark the intonation, circling the arrow on the left (↗) when the speaker is asking a question and wants information; circle the arrow on the right (↘) when the speaker is giving an opinion and wants to know if the other person agrees.

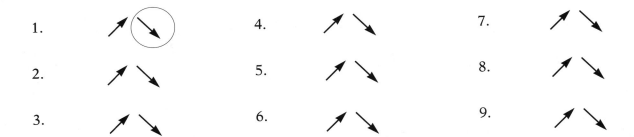

Lesson 7

▶ **Read the article from a school newspaper. Then write a similar article about an interesting place you have visited.**

Colonial Williamsburg

By Lee T. Baron

One of the most interesting places I have ever visited is Williamsburg, Virginia. It dates from 1699 and is one of the oldest towns in the United States.

The town has changed very little over the years. Many houses and buildings are from the eighteenth and nineteenth centuries, and archeologists and architects have restored other parts of the town.

Many streets in the historic town are closed to cars, so it is easy to get around. You can rent a bicycle or ride in a horse-drawn carriage, but most people prefer to walk.

I think I liked the old shops the best. Inside, men and women were making candles, books, jewelry, and baskets, and I saw the kinds of crafts that people made in the eighteenth century. Some of the people who worked in the shops were wearing clothes from that time.

It is easy to get to Williamsburg. By car, it is about three hours from Washington, D.C. Two airports are also nearby. Colonial Williamsburg is open year round, and I think you would enjoy a visit there.

_____

By _____

_____

_____

_____

_____

_____

_____

_____

_____

_____

_____

Lesson 8

▶ **Put the lines of the conversations in order. Then write the conversations.**

1. ____ Didn't you already speak some Chinese when you got here?

____ Not everything. My vocabulary is still limited.

_1_ I'm impressed. When you speak Chinese, you sound like a native.

____ Well, you seem to get along really well.

____ Do you understand everything now?

____ A little. But I had a hard time understanding people.

____ Well, not quite. I still have trouble expressing myself.

A *I'm impressed. When you speak Chinese, you sound like a native.* _____

B _____

A _____

B _____

A _____

B _____

A _____

2. ____ You'll get used to the traffic. Everyone does.

____ Oh, sure, a little at first. But I'm pretty used to it now.

____ So, how do you like living in Taiwan?

____ Look at all those motorcycles! I'm going to have trouble getting across the street.

____ Did you have any trouble getting used to the way of life here?

____ I love it, but I miss seeing my family and friends.

A _____

B _____

A _____

B _____

A _____

B _____

Lesson 9

1 ▶ **Complete the conversations with the sentences in the box.**

> How do you like working here?
> I've worked here for almost a year.
> I like it a lot, but I get homesick at times.
>
> How do you like living so far from home?
> I love it, but I miss some of my coworkers at my old job.
> I've lived here for almost six months.

1. **A** How long have you been with the company?
   B _I've worked here for almost a year._
   A _____
   B _____

2. **A** How long have you been here?
   B _____
   A _____
   B _____

2 ▶ **Listen to the conversations. In each one, someone states a preference. Complete the sentences.**

1. The man would rather _study now,_ _____
2. The man would just as soon _____
3. The woman would just as soon _____
4. The woman would rather _____

3 ▶ **Answer the questions with your own information.**

1. Would you like to go to the movies tonight, or would you rather not go out?
   _____

2. Do you want to get some exercise this weekend, or would you just as soon relax?
   _____

3. Are you interested in traveling to other countries, or would you rather get to know your own country better?
   _____

4. Do you like to eat new foods, or would you just as soon eat things you're used to?
   _____

5. Would you like to work for a large company, or would you rather work for a small one?
   _____

4 ▶ **Paolo has come from Italy to study in the United States. Complete the conversations he's had with people he's met at the university.**

Conversation 1

Amy How long have you been in the U.S.?

Paolo *Three months.* _____

Amy Only three months? Your English is fantastic.

Paolo Well, I studied English in Italy, but _____

_____

Amy Everybody finds it difficult when people talk very fast.

Conversation 2

Charlie How do you like living in the States?

Paolo _____

Charlie I understand. It's hard to be so far from your family. What else is difficult for you here?

Paolo _____

Charlie I know. I don't like to get up for early classes either. No one gets used to that easily.

Conversation 3

Ken How about going into town for dinner tonight? Do you like Mexican food?

Paolo Not too much, actually. _____

Can we go somewhere where the food isn't so spicy?

Ken Sure. How about an Italian restaurant? _____

Paolo No, I don't really. I get so much Italian food in the cafeteria that I don't miss it at all.

5 ▶ **Write sentences about your habits, using *I'm (not) used to* and the ideas in the box.**

Do you usually . . .	
drink coffee after dinner?	get up early during the week?
eat a big breakfast?	sleep late on Sunday?
watch TV during the day?	rent movies at the video store?
take your vacation during the summer?	study with the radio on?

1. _____

2. _____

3. _____

4. _____

5. _____

6. _____

7. _____

8. _____

Lesson 10

1 ► Complete the sentences with *so, such, so much,* or *so many*. Then match the complaints with the reasons.

1. I've got _____*such*_____ a headache.
2. I'm _____ nervous.
3. I have _____ a bad pain in my side.
4. I've got _____ to do tonight.
5. It's hard to drive _____ slowly.

a. I'm not used to speaking in front of _____ people.
b. I'm not used to _____ loud music.
c. I'm not used to driving in _____ heavy rain.
d. Our science teacher gave us _____ homework.
e. I'm not used to running _____ far.

2 ► Complete the conversations, using the sentences in exercise 1.

1. **A** *I've got such a headache.*

   B How come?

   A *I'm not used to such loud music.*

2. **A** _____

   B Why?

   A _____

3. **A** _____

   B I thought you jogged every day.

   A _____

4. **A** _____

   B Oh, don't be.

   A _____

5. **A** _____

   B Well, why are you going only 15 miles
   an hour?

   A _____

Lesson 11

1 ▶ Imagine that you are writing in your journal. Complete this page, writing about three problems you have with the English language.

October 4

Things are going well. I'm learning a lot in my English class, and I feel better about speaking English now. However, I still have some problems. I have trouble

I think I can improve my English if I practice speaking more.

2 ▶ When Larry comes home, Sarah is reading a letter from their son, Bob. Bob is spending a year in Tolo, an isolated island in the Pacific Ocean. Listen to each part of the conversation and write *That's right* or *That's wrong* after each statement.

Part 1

1. This is Bob's second letter from Tolo. *That's wrong.*

2. Bob is teaching sports to Toloese children. _____

3. Bob isn't getting along very well in his job. _____

Part 2

4. The Toloese are good at playing baseball, and they'd rather play it than soccer. _____

5. Bob must not be good at playing gonshu. _____

6. Bob doesn't enjoy being alone. _____

Part 3

7. Bob isn't used to getting up so early. _____

8. Bob teaches early in the morning. _____

9. Bob misses watching TV. _____

Part 4

10. Bob is having trouble learning Toloese. _____

11. Toloese sounds a lot like English. _____

12. Bob isn't homesick. _____

Lesson 12

1 ▶ **Complete the conversation, using *stay* or *staying*.**

A Would you rather _____*stay*_____ here in the hotel or go sightseeing?

B Sightseeing? It's almost ten o'clock at night!

A That's not so late. Lots of people in New York actually _____ up until dawn.

B Well, I'd just as soon _____ here. I'm not used to _____ up late. To tell you the truth, I'm already having trouble _____ awake.

A You used to _____ up late when you were younger, didn't you?

B Oh, sure. People always enjoy _____ up late when they're young.

2 ▶ **Rewrite each sentence, using *so, such, so much,* or *so many*. Change only the underlined words.**

1. He's <u>very</u> tired.
   He's so tired.

2. We aren't used to eating <u>very</u> spicy food.
   _____

3. She speaks English <u>very</u> well.
   _____

4. It was a busy trip, but we enjoyed visiting <u>lots of</u> new places.
   _____

5. I had <u>a lot of</u> trouble when I first started studying English.
   _____

6. Tim and Jim are <u>very</u> good friends.
   _____

3 ▶ **Imagine you are going to the United States for the first time. Complete these sentences with your own information. Use a gerund in each sentence.**

1. On my first day there, I'm thinking of _*visiting my cousin.*_____

2. I think I'll enjoy _____

3. I'm looking forward to _____

4. I'll probably miss _____

5. I don't think I'll be good at _____

6. I might have a hard time _____

Lesson 13

📼 **1** ▶ **Listen to each conversation. Then complete each sentence. Circle *a* or *b*.**

1. She _____ used to eating a big breakfast.
   a. is
   (b.) isn't

2. He's not used to driving _____ .
   a. such long distances
   b. such a large car

3. She _____ going to her favorite café.
   a. misses
   b. is looking forward to

4. He must _____ following directions.
   a. be good at
   b. have trouble

5. They _____ used to living in an apartment.
   a. are
   b. aren't

6. She'd _____ stay home tonight.
   a. just as soon
   b. rather not

📼 **2** ▶ **People often confuse the expression *be used to* with the past expression *used to*. Listen to each sentence and check (✔) the expression you hear.**

	be used to	*used to*
1.	✔	_____
2.	_____	_____
3.	_____	_____
4.	_____	_____
5.	_____	_____
6.	_____	_____
7.	_____	_____
8.	_____	_____

📼 **3** ▶ **Listen to the conversations. Mark the strongest vowel or vowel combination in each sentence. In some sentences, you will mark two strongly stressed vowels.**

☐ ☐ ■ ☐ ■ ☐
1. **A** I've got such a headache!

☐ ☐ ☐ ☐ ☐ ☐ ☐☐
   B Why don't you take some aspirin?

☐ ☐ ☐ ☐ ☐ ☐ ☐☐ ☐ ☐   ☐☐ ☐ ☐ ☐ ☐
   A I'd rather not take aspirin. It gives me a stomachache.

☐ ☐ ☐ ☐ ☐ ☐ ☐☐☐ ☐☐☐ ☐ ☐ ☐☐ ☐ ☐ ☐☐
2. **A** I'm looking forward to taking it easy this weekend. I'm so tired!

☐ ☐ ☐ ☐ ☐☐ ☐ ☐ ☐ ☐ ☐
   B That's because you're not used to working so hard.

☐ ☐ ☐ ☐
   A You're right. I'm not.

Lesson 14

► **Read these letters from the pen-pal page of a magazine. Then write an answer to one of them, telling about yourself.**

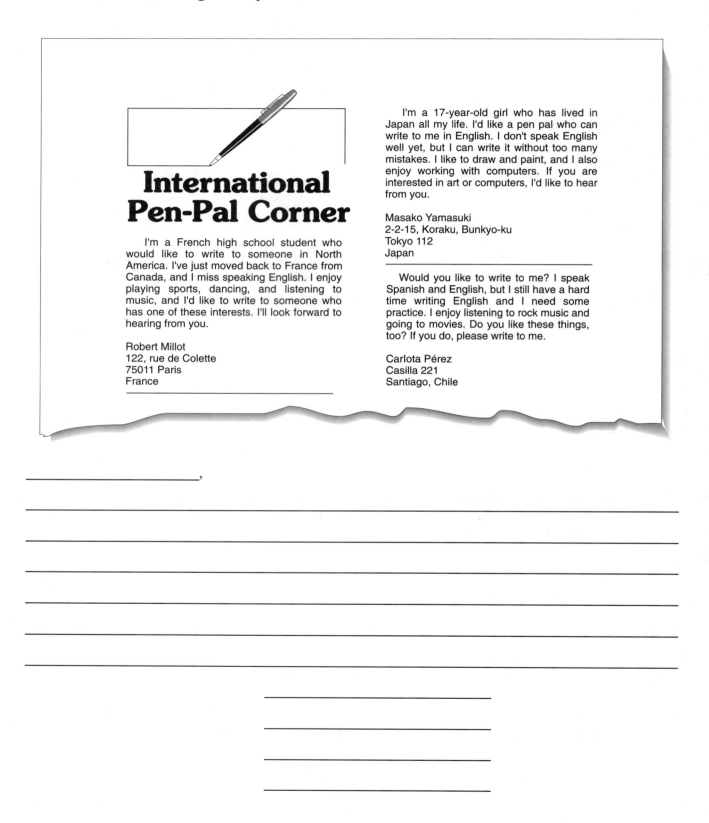

International Pen-Pal Corner

I'm a French high school student who would like to write to someone in North America. I've just moved back to France from Canada, and I miss speaking English. I enjoy playing sports, dancing, and listening to music, and I'd like to write to someone who has one of these interests. I'll look forward to hearing from you.

Robert Millot
122, rue de Colette
75011 Paris
France

I'm a 17-year-old girl who has lived in Japan all my life. I'd like a pen pal who can write to me in English. I don't speak English well yet, but I can write it without too many mistakes. I like to draw and paint, and I also enjoy working with computers. If you are interested in art or computers, I'd like to hear from you.

Masako Yamasuki
2-2-15, Koraku, Bunkyo-ku
Tokyo 112
Japan

Would you like to write to me? I speak Spanish and English, but I still have a hard time writing English and I need some practice. I enjoy listening to rock music and going to movies. Do you like these things, too? If you do, please write to me.

Carlota Pérez
Casilla 221
Santiago, Chile

_____,

_____

_____

_____

_____

_____

_____

_____

_____

_____

_____

Lesson 15

▶ **Read each conversation. Then complete the summary.**

1. **Naomi** Good morning!
   Angie Oh, good morning, Naomi.
   Naomi What are you reading the classifieds for?
   Angie I need someone to take care of my little boy.
   Naomi What kind of person are you looking for?
   Angie Oh, you know, someone who's mature …
   someone who's good with children …
   a responsible person who's willing to make
   dinner if I have to work late.
   Naomi Well, I have a friend whose daughter likes
   to baby-sit. She seems very mature. I'm not
   sure if she can cook, though.

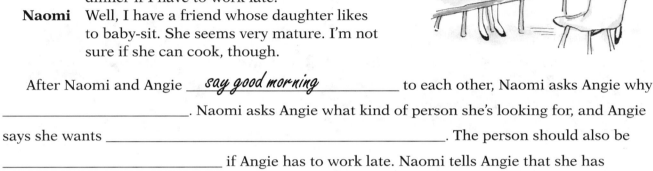

After Naomi and Angie ___*say good morning*___ to each other, Naomi asks Angie why

_____. Naomi asks Angie what kind of person she's looking for, and Angie

says she wants _____. The person should also be

_____ if Angie has to work late. Naomi tells Angie that she has

a friend _____. The friend's daughter

_____, but Naomi isn't sure _____.

2. **Naomi** Aren't you going to lunch, Angie?
   Angie No, I'm not hungry. Besides, I'd rather read my book.
   Naomi *The Joy Luck Club.* … What's it about?
   Angie Well, it's about a group of Chinese women who live
   in San Francisco. The main character is an
   American-born woman whose mother came
   from China.
   Naomi It sounds interesting. Who's it by?
   Angie Amy Tan.
   Naomi She wrote *The Woman Warrior* too, didn't she?
   Angie No, that was written by Maxine Hong Kingston.

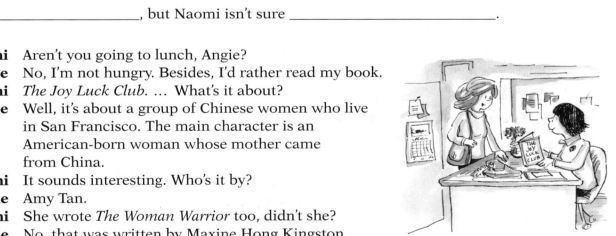

Angie isn't going to lunch because _____ and she _____.

The book is about _____. The main character is

an American-born woman _____. Naomi thinks

the book _____. When she asks who the book _____,

Angie tells her the author's name: Amy Tan. Naomi thinks Amy Tan wrote *The Woman Warrior*

too, but Angie tells her _____.

Lesson 16

1 ▶ **Match the people in Column A with the works and places in Column B. Then look at the answers at the bottom of the page.**

1. Andrew Lloyd Webber
2. Pedro Alvares Cabral
3. Stephen King
4. Steven Spielberg
5. Walt Disney
6. Georgia O'Keeffe
7. Shah Jahan
8. Alexander Graham Bell

a. Brazil
b. the Taj Mahal
c. the movie *Jurassic Park*
d. the telephone
e. Mickey Mouse and Donald Duck
f. the novels *The Shining* and *Needful Things*
g. the painting *Black and Purple Petunias*
h. the musicals *Phantom of the Opera* and *Cats*

2 ▶ **Complete the conversations, using the information in exercise 1.**

1. **A** Martin Scorsese directed the movie *Jurassic Park*, didn't he?
   B *No, Jurassic Park was directed by Steven Spielberg.*

2. **A** Christopher Columbus discovered Brazil, didn't he?
   B _____

3. **A** Thomas Edison invented the telephone, didn't he?
   B _____

4. **A** Van Gogh painted *Black and Purple Petunias*, didn't he?
   B _____

5. **A** Charles Schulz created Mickey Mouse and Donald Duck, didn't he?
   B _____

6. **A** Roger Daltry composed *Phantom of the Opera* and *Cats*, didn't he?
   B _____

7. **A** Louis XIV built the Taj Mahal, didn't he?
   B _____

8. **A** Mary Higgins Clark wrote *The Shining* and *Needful Things*, didn't she?
   B _____

Answers: 2. a   3. f   4. c   5. e
6. g   7. b   8. d

18 Unit 3

3 ► **Read the newspaper article. Then rewrite it, changing the parts in brackets [ ] to the passive and omitting the agent where it isn't necessary.**

Fire Damages Historic Building

[An early-morning fire damaged the historic Geller House] today. [It destroyed the third floor of the building], but [firefighters saved the first and second floors]. There were only a few elderly residents in the building at the time, and [people carried them] to safety.

[They built the Geller House] in 1718, and [they used it] as a hotel for over 150 years. George Washington stayed there in 1782. [The Geller family owned the building] until the 1930s. Then [they sold it] to the Mills family. Several years ago, [they made it] into an apartment building for the elderly.

[They called several fire departments] to the scene. When [we asked Fire Chief Andrew Barnes] how the fire started, he answered that most likely [a burning cigarette caused it]. Chief Barnes promised a complete investigation.

The historic Geller House was damaged by an early-morning fire today.

_____

_____

_____

_____

_____

_____

_____

_____

_____

_____

_____

_____

4 ► **Complete the conversation, giving news and reacting to it.**

A I got a letter from Elena today.

B Really? How are she and Charlie doing?

A Well, there's some good news and some bad news. First, the bad news. *Charlie was laid off a couple of weeks ago,* _____ His company doesn't have much work right now.

B _____ I know he loved his job. What's he going to do now?

A He has to look for another job, of course. But there's good news too. _____ _____ She was in the sales department at L&B, and now she's the manager.

B _____ I'm sure Elena will be an excellent manager.

Lesson 17

1 ▶ **Complete the conversation with *who, who's,* or *whose.***

A ___Who's___ that? The man over there in the hat _____ looks like a cowboy?

B I don't know. Do you know _____ he is, Paula?

C Sure. That's the man I was telling you about. He's the one _____ wife is an actress and _____ family just moved into the neighborhood.

B Oh, yeah. Isn't he the one _____ just came back from a year in Australia and _____ writing a book about his experiences?

A I think so. And _____ that in the raincoat? Doesn't he look familiar?

B Yes. He looks like that TV detective _____ always wears a raincoat and _____ hair is always messy.

C Oh, I know _____ you're talking about. I don't think that's really him, though.

2 ▶ **Two neighbors are looking at the bulletin board in the supermarket. Complete their conversation about the want ads.**

> WANTED
>
> Mature, experienced baby-sitter for my 3-year-old son. Willing to work weekdays, 9-12.
>
> Call Mrs. Lewis at 555-0166.

> WANTED
> Responsible person to rent my apartment for the summer. Reasonable rate. Must like cats — I have six of them! Joe Zwick, 555-4213 (eves.)

A Look, there's an ad over here by Mrs. Lewis. *She's looking for a baby-sitter for her son.*

B What kind of person is she looking for?

A _____

_____

B I may know of someone. I think I'll call Mrs. Lewis later. ...Oh, Joe Zwick put up a notice, too.

A He did? How come?

B _____

A Does he say what kind of person he wants?

B _____

Lesson 18

1 ▶ **Some friends are talking about their plans for the evening. Complete the conversations, using the information in the box. In the first conversation, write the questions. In the second, write the answers.**

> 1. *Madame Butterfly* is an opera by Giacomo Puccini. It's about a Japanese woman. Her American husband has to leave her and go back to the United States.
>
> 2. *A Doll's House* is a play by Henrik Ibsen. It's about a Norwegian woman. Her husband doesn't want her to grow up.

1. **A** *What are you going to do tonight?*

   B We're going to see the opera *Madame Butterfly*.

   A _____

   B Giacomo Puccini.

   A _____

   B A Japanese woman whose American husband has to leave her and go back to the States.

2. **A** What are you going to do tonight?

   B _____

   A Who's it by?

   B _____

   A What's it about?

   B _____

2 ▶ **Listen to each conversation. Write the number on the picture that shows a scene from the book or play the people are talking about.**

Lesson 19

1 ▶ **Read the sentences. Then write a definition for each of the underlined words, using *who*, *who's*, or *whose*.**

1. Sam is a <u>good-for-nothing</u>. He is dishonest and does no work.
   A good-for-nothing is someone who's dishonest and who does no work.

2. Andy is a <u>pacifist</u>. He believes that all wars are wrong.
   _____
   _____

3. Chuck is a <u>lumberjack</u>. His job is to cut down trees for wood.
   _____
   _____

4. Most successful politicians are <u>orators</u>; they can speak very well in front of large groups.
   _____
   _____

5. Poor Mrs. Lee! Her husband has died, so now she's a <u>widow</u>.
   _____
   _____

6. Mark is a <u>philatelist</u>. His hobby is collecting stamps.
   _____
   _____

7. Dr. Wong is a <u>podiatrist</u>. He specializes in foot problems.
   _____
   _____

8. Clara is an <u>octogenarian</u>. She's between 80 and 90 years old.
   _____
   _____

2 ▶ **Write about six famous inventions, discoveries, works, or places, using the passive in the past tense. Use the ideas in the box or your own ideas.**

The Chinese invented paper. William Shakespeare wrote *Romeo and Juliet*.
A British prisoner named William Addis invented the toothbrush. The Incas built Machu Picchu almost 500 years ago.
Sir Alexander Fleming discovered penicillin. Frank Lloyd Wright designed Tokyo's Imperial Hotel.

1. _____
2. _____
3. _____
4. _____
5. _____
6. _____

Lesson 20

1 ► **Listen to each conversation. Then answer the questions, using your own words. Don't try to write every word you hear.**

Conversation 1

1. Why doesn't Shelley like her apartment?

_____

2. What's Shelley's news?

_____

Conversation 2

3. What is Shelley doing when Bert arrives?

_____

4. What kind of person is she looking for?

_____

5. What is Bert going to give Shelley?

_____

2 ► **Listen and complete each conversation with *a* or *b*.**

1. a. I'm glad to hear that. That's really good news.
   b. I'm sorry to hear that. That's really too bad.

2. a. No. They were invented by Thomas Edison.
   b. I'm not sure who invented it.

3. a. Yes, she did.
   b. Yes, it was.

4. a. Oh, I'm sorry to hear that.
   b. Oh, good for her.

5. a. Someone who likes animals.
   b. Someone who's good with children.

6. a. It was built by the Incas.
   b. It was built during the fifteenth century.

3 ► **Listen to the sentences and check (✔) the words you hear.**

	who	*who's*	*whose*
1.	✔		
2.			
3.			
4.			
5.			
6.			
7.			
8.			

Lesson 21

▶ **Read the movie review. Then write a similar review about a movie you've seen or a book you've read recently.**

The Fugitive

The Fugitive is based on the old TV show of the same name, but the movie is better than the show ever was. When Dr. Richard Kimble (played by Harrison Ford) is falsely accused of murdering his wife, he runs from the police. In order to prove his innocence, he must find the one-armed man he knows is his wife's real killer. A lawman named Sam Gerard (played by Tommy Lee Jones) is determined to find Kimble and make him pay for the crime that he did not commit. As Kimble escapes time and time again, Gerard becomes angrier and more frustrated.

The Fugitive was written by Jeb Stuart and David Twohy, and directed by Andrew Davis. To say any more about this thrilling action film would be unfair to the viewer. It's a movie you won't forget.

Don't miss it.

_____

_____

_____

_____

_____

_____

_____

_____

_____

Lesson 22

▶ **Complete the conversation with the sentences in the box.**

> Tuesdays and Fridays are out for me.
> Lynn's going to be late.
> I can look it up for you in my address book.
> Please, anything but pizza.
> Oh, he can't make it. Any evening but Monday's O.K. with him.
> Well, I'll try. I just wish I'd known earlier.
> Why don't we meet right after work on Thursday?
> Wait! I have a dentist appointment at 5:30.
> Everyone except David is.
> I'm busy all Saturday afternoon.

A Let's see … who's missing?

B *Lynn's going to be late.* _____

A Is everybody else here?

C _____

A Does anyone know if he's coming?

D _____

A So that leaves Tuesdays, Thursdays, and Fridays.

E _____

D Couldn't we do it on the weekend?

B _____

C And I'm busy the whole day.

F _____

B That's fine with me. We could order a pizza.

E _____

B So will everyone be able to come this Thursday at about six?

E _____

B Could you possibly change it to some other day?

E _____

B So Thursday it is. Does anyone happen to know David's phone number?

A _____

Lesson 23

1 ▶ Look at the class attendance sheet and write sentences about each day of the week. Vary your answers, using the words in the box. (A check means the student was there.)

everybody everyone but except nobody no one						

NAME	Monday	Tuesday	Wednesday	Thursday	Friday
Chang Lee	✔	✔	✔		
Mirta Lopez	✔		✔		
Robert Williams	✔	✔	✔		✔
Walter Stein		✔	✔		
Doris Smith	✔		✔		
Iris Goldberg	✔	✔	✔		
Carlo Luciano	✔	✔	✔		

1. *On Monday, everyone was there except Walter.*
2. _____
3. _____
4. _____
5. _____

2 ▶ Read the information given and then complete each conversation. Use an indefinite compound and *except* or *but*.

1. Rosa went to a party on Saturday. She knew only her friend Marcy.

   Bob Did you know everybody at the party?
   Rosa *I didn't know anybody except Marcy.*

2. Thad is having lunch at a friend's house. He hates tuna fish, but he likes everything else.

   Sue Why don't we have tuna fish sandwiches for lunch?
   Thad _____

3. Ginny is talking to a friend at the gym. She likes to exercise after work, but she's only free on Thursday evenings.

   Linda Do you come here every evening after work?
   Ginny _____

4. There are four Japanese restaurants in town. Thad likes Japanese food, but he's only been to one of the restaurants, the Japanese Inn.

   Lee Let's have dinner. Have you been to all of the Japanese restaurants?
   Thad _____

5. Some of Evelyn's classmates want to study together Tuesday morning. Evelyn is free only on Saturday morning.

   Chuck Some of us are getting together to study Tuesday morning. Would you like to join us?
   Evelyn _____

3 ▶ Read the list—it shows the information Mark needs to find out. Before he calls the people on the list, Mark's coworker Stan tells him that he's just talked on the phone to each of the people. Write Mark's questions and Stan's answers.

MARK HIGGINS

Find out if:
- Paul is coming to the meeting this afternoon.
- Sue can type the weekly report tomorrow.
- Debra is going to the company picnic with Stan and me.
- Ron is going to meet Stan and me for lunch.

Paul: I can't make it. Please call me after the meeting.

Sue: I'll do it first thing tomorrow. Please leave it on my desk.

Debra: I'm looking forward to it. Don't forget to pick me up.

Ron: I'll be a little late. Don't wait for me.

1. **Mark** _Do you know if Paul is coming to the meeting this afternoon?_
   Stan _He can't make it. He said to call him after the meeting._

2. **Mark** _____
   Stan _____

3. **Mark** _____
   Stan _____

4. **Mark** _____
   Stan _____

4 ▶ Listen to each conversation and circle the correct words.

1. He (eats, doesn't eat) vegetables.
2. She (likes, doesn't like) to swim.
3. They (should, shouldn't) wait for Kim.
4. Kathy (was, wasn't) at the dance.
5. He (wants, doesn't want) to see a horror movie.
6. (Everybody, Nobody) was in class tonight.
7. (No one, Everyone) was wrong.
8. They decide to get together on (Tuesday, Thursday).

Lesson 24

1 ▶ **Some people are trying to plan a play rehearsal. Complete the conversation.**

A We'd like to have our first rehearsal Friday evening. Can all of you make it?

B *That's fine with me.* _____ I'm free every Friday all summer.

A Great. Jeff?

C _____

A O.K. Let me know as soon as possible. How about you, Carol?

D _____ My work schedule was changed yesterday, so Fridays are out.

A Oh, that's really too bad.

D _____

A We didn't know earlier. We just decided this morning. But now we might have to choose another time.

2 ▶ **You are trying to plan a picnic with some of your friends. Write each underlined sentence another way, using *the whole, this whole, all,* or *every.***

A When can we get together?

B I already have plans for the evenings this week.
I already have plans every evening this week.

C Me too. I'm busy the whole week.

_____

A I guess that leaves the weekend.

D I can't make it this Saturday. I'll be at my sister's all day.

_____

A O.K. Saturday's out. Sunday?

B Sunday's good. I'm free the whole day.

_____

D I always baby-sit on Sunday mornings, but I'm free all afternoon.

_____

3 ▶ Complete the conversation with *might (not)/will (not) be able to.*

A Brendan, you *'ll be able to* _____ come to the picnic on Sunday, won't you?

B Oh, didn't I tell you? I _____ make it. I have to work all day Sunday.

A I'm really sorry to hear that. Do you know if Erica _____ come?

B She really wants to go, but she _____. She _____

get a ride.

A Oh, Joe and I _____ give her a ride. Tell her we'll pick her up at noon.

4 ▶ Match the information in Column A with the places in Column B
where the information could be found.

A	**B**
1. Pam's phone number	a. the phone book
2. what's on TV tonight	b. the dictionary
3. the country code for Greece	c. the newspaper
4. the capital of Thailand	d. my address book
5. how to pronounce t-r-e-a-c-h-e-r-y	e. the atlas

5 ▶ A friend is asking you for the information in exercise 4. Write
the conversations. If you know the information, be sure to say so.

1. **A** *Do you happen to know Pam's phone number?*
   B *Not offhand, but I can look it up for you in my address book.*

2. **A** _____
   B _____

3. **A** _____
   B _____

4. **A** _____
   B _____

5. **A** _____
   B _____

Lesson 25

1 ▶ **Choose the sentence that means the same or almost the same. Circle *a* or *b*.**

1. She's busy Friday evening, but she doesn't have plans any other evening.

    (a.) She's free every evening except Friday.

    b. She isn't free any evening but Friday.

2. I have to work every day this week except Saturday.

    a. I'll be out on Saturday.

    b. I'm off on Saturday.

3. He's free all afternoon.

    a. He's free the whole afternoon.

    b. He's free every afternoon.

4. We can't go.

    a. We may not go.

    b. We won't be able to make it.

5. The library is the only place I can't study.

    a. I can study anywhere but the library.

    b. I can't study anywhere but the library.

2 ▶ **Imagine someone asks you the following questions. Write responses, using your own information.**

1. Have you been to every class so far?

    _____

2. We're having a party next Friday afternoon. Can you be there?

    _____

3. Let's get together next Tuesday. How does 6:30 in the evening sound?

    _____

4. Do you happen to know what the word *curiosity* means?

    _____

5. What should we have for dinner tomorrow night?

    _____

6. When you do your English homework, does it take you the whole evening?

    _____

Lesson 26

1 ▶ **Listen to each conversation and complete it with the best response from the box.**

1. _b_   5. _____
2. _____   6. _____
3. _____   7. _____
4. _____   8. _____

> a. They're busy the whole weekend.
> b. We ran into each other at the post office.
> c. She said to save her some meatloaf.
> d. Actually, I don't want anything. I'm not hungry.
> e. Then how about the Carlsons?
> f. They're busy every weekend.
> g. Then how about Friday night?
> h. He said not to order the meatloaf.

2 ▶ **Listen to the conversations and answer the questions with *Yes* or *No*.**

1. Is Ana there? _No,_
2. Is anyone missing? _____
3. Does the woman want tuna fish? _____
4. Did they serve cheese at the party? _____
5. Can the man study for the test on Tuesday? _____
6. Should they wait for Terry? _____
7. Should they wait for Wanda? _____
8. Is the man busy on Wednesdays? _____
9. Is the woman busy the whole week? _____
10. Will the man be able to go to the next volleyball practice? _____

3 ▶ **Listen to the conversation. Then look at the receptionist's calendar and write down when Steve Green and his children, Sally and Todd, have their appointments with the dentist.**

WEEK-AT-A-GLANCE CALENDAR

	Monday March 21	Tuesday March 22	Wednesday March 23	Thursday March 24	Friday March 25
9:00					
9:30					
10:00					
10:30					
11:00					
11:30					
12:00					
12:30					
1:00					
1:30					
2:00					
2:30					
3:00					
3:30					
4:00					
4:30					
5:00					

Lesson 27

▶ You have received an invitation to your friend Arthur's wedding. Write him a letter, telling him that you can't attend the wedding. Apologize and explain why you won't be able to go.

Mr. and Mrs. Carlos Blanco
request the honor of your presence
at the wedding of their daughter
Elvira Aida Blanco
to Mr. Arthur Fletcher Carruthers
at four o'clock in the afternoon
on the twentieth of December
at their residence,
23 Oak Grove Road
R.S.V.P.

_____ ,

_____

_____

_____

_____

_____

_____

_____

_____ ,

_____

Review of units 1-4

1 ▶ Rebecca Watson isn't sure what she should study in college. Her counselor asked her to make a list of her strengths, weaknesses, likes, and dislikes. Look at Rebecca's list and then complete the sentences, using a gerund in each answer.

* like to learn about other countries
* can learn languages easily
* would like to travel during vacations
* can't use a computer very well
* can't learn math easily
* always study hard

1. I have always enjoyed *learning about other countries.* _____

2. I'm good at _____

3. I'm looking forward to _____

4. I have trouble _____

5. I have a hard time _____

6. I'm used to _____

2 ▶ Rebecca is spending her spring vacation in Paris, France. Complete her postcard, using the superlative form of the adjectives and the present perfect of the verbs in parentheses.

Dear Mom and Dad,

Well, here I am in Paris! The flight was a little scary – in fact, it was <u>the worst flight I've ever been on</u> (bad, be on). Definitely _____ (bumpy, take)! Anyway, we landed early in the morning and took a taxi to the hotel. This city is so incredibly beautiful – it's _____ _____ (beautiful, see). We had a few hours' sleep, and then we went out for lunch. The restaurant wasn't very expensive, but the food was _____ (delicious, have). You know how much I love french fries. Well, the ones we had at lunch were _____ (good, taste). I have to go now. We're off to the Eiffel Tower! À bientôt! (That's French for "See you soon.")

Rebecca

3 ▶ There were several robberies on Rebecca's street while she was away. Combine the sentences with *whose* and change the second sentence to the passive.

1. There are several families on this street. Someone broke into their houses during the night.
   <u>*There are several families on this street whose houses were broken into*</u>
   <u>*during the night.*</u>

2. Patricia Rojas is one neighbor. They robbed her house.
   _____
   _____

3. Emil Williams is a neighbor. They stole his TV and CD player.
   _____
   _____

4. Andrea and Paul Stein are neighbors. Someone took their jewelry.
   _____
   _____

4 ▶ Rewrite the first parts of the sentences in the box, using *so* or *such*, and match them with their appropriate endings.

It's really cold out …	His cooking is terrible …
A lot of people came to the play …	It was a great movie …
He did good work …	

1. <u>*So many people came to the play*</u> that the actors were very nervous.
2. _____ that our car won't start.
3. _____ that he was promoted.
4. _____ that I went to see it again.
5. _____ that even he can't eat it.

5 ▶ Answer the questions with complete sentences, using your own information.

1. Are all the students in your English class from the same country?
   _____

2. Is there anyone in your class who has a very interesting job? What does he/she do?
   _____

3. When your teacher gives you advice that will help you learn English faster and more easily, what does he/she say to do? What does he/she say not to do?
   _____
   _____
   _____

Lesson 28

▶ **Put the lines of the conversations in order. Then write the conversations.**

1. ____ It was painted by a young Nigerian artist.

   ____ Hey, look at those fabulous prints.

   _1_ What a wonderful painting!

   ____ You seem to have a lot of things from Africa.

   ____ Those are woodblocks. They're made in Japan.

   ____ Well, my husband's Nigerian. Our daughter was born
   and brought up in Lagos.

A _What a wonderful painting!_

B _____

A _____

B _____

C _____

B _____

2. ____ Oh, really? I was a hairstylist before I got married.

   ____ I work for a construction company, and Donna's a hairstylist.

   ____ Do you ever miss styling hair?

   ____ Well, if I had more time, I'd travel more.

   ____ You were saying that you used to be a hairstylist.

   ____ Oh, yes.

   ____ What do you folks do?

   ____ Excuse me, Mom. You have a phone call.

   ____ Sometimes. If I had more time, I'd open a small hair salon.

   ____ Will you excuse me? … I'm sorry. Now, what were we talking about?

B _____

C _____

B _____

D _____

B _____

C _____

B _____

A _____

B _____

A _____

Lesson 29

1 ▶ **Find the two conversations. Then write the conversations next to the correct pictures.**

1 **A** We took a cruise last month.

2 **A** We rented a house on the beach last weekend.

____ **B** Oh, really? How was the trip?

____ **B** Oh, really? Did you enjoy it?

____ **A** We had a lot of fun. But while we were there, the electricity went out.

____ **A** We had a great time. But during the trip, there was a big storm.

1. **A** _____

   B _____

   A _____

   _____

2. **A** _____

   B _____

   A _____

   _____

2 ▶ **Complete the phrases with *while* or *during*. Then complete each conversation with a phrase from the box.**

during the soccer match	_____ we were on vacation
_____ the meal	_____ I was at the movies
_____ we were at rehearsal	

1. **A** What happened to you?

   B I broke my leg _____*during the soccer match*_____. The worst part is that the other team won!

2. **A** How was your dinner last night?

   B Not too good. _____, I got sick and had to go home.

3. **A** You look so relaxed!

   B I am. The trip really helped. We both got plenty of good food, rest, and exercise _____.

4. **A** I called you and Phil last night, but no one answered.

   B Several people called _____. The play is really taking up all our time.

5. **A** You look depressed.

   B I am. Last night somebody stole my car _____.
   And the movie was about a robbery, too!

Lesson 30

▶ **Andrew Barnes's mother recently gave him some old photographs. Complete the paragraph about Andrew's life experiences, using the information next to the pictures. Write one word in each blank.**

Andrew John Barnes, one week old
Bennington, Vermont
12/17/40

The move to Wilmington
5/7/49

Andrew and Janet O'Hara
High school graduation
6/23/59

Andrew and Janet's wedding
8/4/59

Janet and Andrew leave for Delmar
10/10/59

Andrew's first day at work
10/15/59

Peggy, one week old
7/9/65

Andrew after his promotion
8/16/89

Andrew Barnes was __*born*__ in Bennington, Vermont, _____ December 10, 1940. He grew _____ there and in _____. Andrew's family _____ to Wilmington _____ Andrew _____ eight years old. Andrew met his _____, Janet O'Hara, in high school, and they got _____ the summer after they graduated. In 1959, Andrew and _____ moved to Delmar, New York, and Andrew _____ working as a firefighter. Janet and Andrew _____ their first child, Peggy, in _____ 1965. In August 1989, after almost _____ years as a firefighter, Andrew was _____ to Fire Chief.

Lesson 31

1 ▶ **Complete the conversations.**

1. **A** I'm so busy these days. But *if I had more time, I'd travel.*

   B Really? Where would you go?

   A I'd probably go to Greece.

2. **A** _____

   B What language would you learn?

   A Spanish, probably. I've always wanted to study it.

3. **A** I'm really broke.

   B What would you do if you had more money?

   A _____

   B A boat? You don't even know how to swim!

4. **A** If I had more money, I'd fix up my apartment.

   B _____

   A I'd buy all new furniture.

2 ▶ **Listen to the conversation and number the pictures in the order you hear the girls talk about their wishes.**

3 ▶ **Complete the sentences with your own information.**

1. If I had a lot of money, _____

   _____

2. If I had more free time, _____

   _____

3. If I had three wishes, _____

   _____

Lesson 32

1 ► **Rewrite this restaurant review, changing the parts in brackets to the passive and omitting the agent where it isn't necessary.**

Rachel's Restaurant Guide

Ratings: * poor to fair   ** good   *** very good   **** excellent

GARDEN OF DELIGHT   Rating: ***
219 Maple Avenue   Tel.: 555-8189
Hours: Lunch, Tues.-Fri. 11:00-2:00
           Dinner, Tues.-Fri. 5:00-9:00, Fri. & Sat. 5:00-10:00

Enter the Garden of Delight, and [something takes you back] to an earlier time. The restaurant used to be a private home. [They built it] in the 1890s. Inside, [they place candles and fresh flowers] on each table. One wall is brick, and the others are painted a soft green.

The food is contemporary, though. [They make everything] with only natural ingredients. [They serve no meat.] [They add no sugar or salt] to any dish.

I ordered calzone. [They filled it] with nuts and mushrooms, and [they covered it] with a bright red vegetable sauce. Unusual and excellent!

I like this place very much. [Owner and chef Peggy Barnes makes everything] in the tiny kitchen. [Waitresses greet you] with friendly smiles. And the prices are very reasonable.

Enter the Garden of Delight, and you are taken back to an earlier time.

_____

_____

_____

_____

_____

_____

_____

_____

_____

_____

2 ► **As you listen to each conversation, correct the statements below.**

1. The students are given homework three times a week.
   The students are given homework four times a week.

2. The man's watch was made in Switzerland.

_____

3. Tickets for the concert are sold only at the stadium.

_____

4. The bread is baked fresh once a day.

_____

5. The woman says that 80% of the world's rice is grown in Asia.

_____

6. Someone in the U.S. is hurt in a car accident every 9 seconds.

_____

Lesson 33

1 ► Look at the names of the products in the box and decide if they are produced, manufactured, raised, or grown. Write each word in the correct column. (Some words can go into more than one column.)

cars	potatoes
cattle	rice
clothes	sheep
coffee	shoes
computers	soap
jewelry	sugar
movies	watches
oil	

Produced	Manufactured	Raised	Grown
cars	*cars*		

2 ► Write sentences about eight of the products in exercise 1, saying where each one is produced, manufactured, raised, or grown. If you need help, look at the map on page 53 of your textbook for information about most of the products.

1. *Cars are manufactured in Japan, the U.S., and Germany.*

2. _____

3. _____

4. _____

5. _____

6. _____

7. _____

8. _____

Lesson 34

🔲 **1** ▶ **Listen and choose the sentence that means the same or almost the same as the sentence you hear. Circle *a* or *b*.**

1. a. Who did that wonderful painting?
   b. That's a wonderful painting.

2. a. Our son grew up in Rio de Janeiro.
   b. We brought our son to Rio de Janeiro.

3. a. Where are those prints from?
   b. Where are those prints?

4. a. She got sick at the airport.
   b. She got sick before she got to the airport.

5. a. He called twice while he was on vacation.
   b. He called twice when he got back from vacation.

6. a. What did you tell me?
   b. What were you saying?

🔲 **2** ▶ **Listen to the conversations and mark the strongest vowel or vowel combinations in the sentences. In some sentences, you will mark more than one strongly stressed vowel sound.**

    □   □   □ ■□ □ □ □ □□ □ □ ■

1. **A** What would you do if you had all the time in the world?

    □ □ □ □□ □□ □ □   □

    B I think I'd travel to other countries.

      □   □ □   □   □ □□

    A Which countries would you visit?

    □ □ □ □□ □ □ □□   □   □ □□□

    B I'd try to see every country in South America.

    □   □   □ □□ □ □ □ □ □ □

2. **A** What would you do if you had lots of money?

    □ □ □ □ □ □□□ □ □□□□ □□□

    B First, I'd give big contributions to my favorite charities.

    □   □   □   □   □ □

    A And then what would you do?

    □ □ □ □ □   □   □ □ □ □   □

    B Then I'd buy a big house with a swimming pool!

Lesson 35

► Imagine that a local newspaper, *Neighborhood News*, had a contest and you won second prize. You and the first-prize winner were both interviewed. Read the answers the first-prize winner gave to the reporter. Then write your answers to the reporter's questions.

Cynthia Hertz has won the *Neighborhood News* first prize of $10,000. Our reporter recently interviewed her at her home.

Reporter: Have you always lived here?

Hertz: I was born in Arizona, but I moved to Houston when I was five years old. I lived there until I went to North Texas State College and met my husband. Then we moved here to North Dallas. We live on Pleasant Hill Lane now.

Reporter: Do you have any other family here?

Hertz: Yes, we have two small children: a boy and a girl. My mother also moved here after my father died. She lives down the street from us. The rest of my family is still in Houston and Arizona.

Reporter: What are you going to do with the $10,000?

Hertz: I always said, "If I had more money, I'd buy new carpeting for my house and I'd travel." And that's what I plan to do with the money.

Our second-prize winner, who received $5,000, was also interviewed. Here's what was said:

Reporter: Have you always lived here?

_____

_____

_____

_____

Reporter: Do you have any other family here?

_____

_____

_____

Reporter: What are you going to do with the $5,000?

_____

_____

_____

_____

_____

Lesson 36

▶ **Read each conversation. Then complete the summary.**

1. **Rachel** I'm going downtown to run some errands. Can I get either of you anything while I'm out?
   Amy Do you think you might go by a post office?
   Rachel I could. What would you like?
   Amy Could you have them weigh this package? Oh, and while you're there, could you get me a book of first-class stamps?
   Rachel Sure. I'd be glad to.
   Kevin If you happen to go by a drugstore, could you have them fill this prescription?
   Rachel Sure. No problem.
   Kevin Here's a twenty-dollar bill. Oh, and would you mind mailing these letters?
   Rachel Not at all.

Rachel is going downtown _____*to run some errands*_____, so she asks her coworkers if she can _____ while she's out. Amy asks her if _____ because she wants Rachel to _____ a package. She'd also like Rachel to get her _____. Then Rachel's coworker Kevin asks her, "_____?" and Rachel answers, "_____." Kevin gives her a _____ and then asks if she _____ mailing some letters. Rachel answers, "_____."

2. **Rachel** I'd like to have some film developed.
   Salesperson O.K. Will there be anything else?
   Rachel While I'm here, I might as well get a roll of film.
   Salesperson Here you are. That'll be $5.35.
   Rachel By the way, is there a drugstore near here?
   Salesperson There's one on Fourth and Main. It's about a ten-minute walk.
   Rachel And what about a post office?
   Salesperson There's one on Fifth and Main.

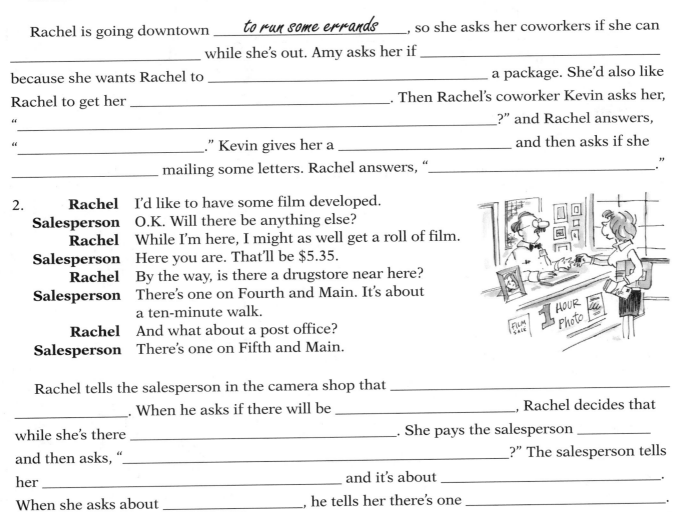

Rachel tells the salesperson in the camera shop that _____. When he asks if there will be _____, Rachel decides that while she's there _____. She pays the salesperson _____ and then asks, "_____?" The salesperson tells her _____ and it's about _____. When she asks about _____, he tells her there's one _____.

Lesson 37

1 ► **Complete the conversations with the sentences in the box.**

> Do you think you might go by a drugstore?
> Could you have them weigh this package?
> Could you have the car washed? It really dirty.
> Do you think you might go by a car wash?
> I'd like to have him fix these pants.
> Do you think you might go by a post office?
> I need to have this prescription filled.
> Are you going anywhere near Tom the Tailor?

1. **A** I'm going into town. Can I get you anything?

   B *Do you think you might go by a post office?*

   A I could. What would you like?

   B _____

   A Sure. No problem.

2. **A** I'm going downtown. Is there anything you need?

   B _____

   A I might. What would you like?

   B _____

   A I can do that for you.

3. **A** I'm going to the dry cleaner's. Is there anything else I should do while I'm out?

   B _____

   A I could. Why?

   B _____

   A Sure.

4. **A** I'm going to the laundromat. Can I do anything for you while I'm out?

   B _____

   A I guess so. How come?

   B _____

   A O.K., sure.

2 ► **Look at the pictures and complete each sentence. Write a sentence using the causative *have* and an active or passive verb form.**

1.

2.

RITA MONDELLO
TO DO:
First thing
Monday —
tell Lisa to type
my report.

3.

CLARK

4.

ROBINSON

PAINT   PAINT

1. Larry is going to *have his hair cut.* _____

2. Rita is going to _____

3. The Clarks should _____

4. The Robinsons are going to _____

3 ► **If you had lots of money, you could have other people do things for you. What would you have them do? Write six sentences using the causative *have* and an active or passive verb form.**

1. *I'd have my house cleaned every day.* _____

2. _____

3. _____

4. _____

5. _____

6. _____

Lesson 38

1 ► **Complete the conversations.**

1. **A** I'm going out to run some errands. Can I get you anything while I'm out?
   B *If you happen to go by a newsstand, could you get me a newspaper?* _____
   A Sure. There's a newsstand right near where I'm going. Which paper would you like: the *Journal* or the *Times*?
   B The *Journal*. _____
   A Don't worry about it. You can pay me when I get back.

2. **A** I'm going to the dry cleaner's.
   B _____
   A Not at all. I'd be glad to. Do you have the receipt for your suit?
   B It's right here. _____
   A Thanks. I'm sure ten dollars will be enough.

2 ► **Complete the puzzle to form noun compounds. When you're finished, you should find another noun compound in the box.**

1. N I N E T E E N - I N C H television
2. ___ ___-___ ___ ___ ___ ___ ___ ___ apartment
3. ___ ___-___ ___ ___ ___ flight
4. ___-___ ___ ___-___ ___ ___ ___ stamp
5. ___ ___ ___ ___ ___ ___ student
6. ___ ___ ___-___ ___ ___ ___ ___
7. ___ ___ ___-___ ___ ___ ___ ___ carton
8. ___ ___ ___ ___ ___ ___ ___ ___
9. ___ ___-___ ___ ___ vacation
10. ___ ___ ___ ___-___ ___ ___ weekend

Clues

1. TV sets come in odd sizes. He couldn't decide between the one that's seventeen inches or the one that's two inches larger. He finally decided on the larger one. He bought a _____.
2. Her apartment has two bedrooms, but it's too expensive. She needs a cheaper, smaller apartment, so she's looking for a _____.
3. If you leave at 6:15, you'll be in Boston at 10:15. It's a _____.
4. This stamp costs seven cents less than a twenty-nine-cent stamp. It's a _____.
5. She's going to college next year, but now she's still a _____.
6. You can mail letters and packages at a _____.
7. A half gallon of milk costs $1.29, and a gallon costs $1.89. He drinks a lot of milk and wants to save money. He's buying a _____.
8. You can buy magazines and newspapers at a _____.
9. I was away for a week and three days. In other words, I took a _____.
10. Many national holidays in the United States are celebrated on Monday, giving people a _____.

Lesson 39

1 ▶ **Follow the conversations. Mark the box next to the sentence you hear.**

1. **A** ■ I'm going downtown.
   A ☐ I'm going into town.
   A ☐ Can I get you anything while I'm out?
   A ☐ Is there anything you need while I'm out?
   B ☐ Do you think you might go by a post office?
   B ☐ Will you be anywhere near a post office?
   A ☐ I could. What do you need?
   A ☐ I could. What would you like?
   B ☐ Would you have them weigh this package?
   B ☐ Could you have them weigh this package?
   A ☐ Sure. I'd be glad to. Anything else?
   A ☐ Sure. No problem. Anything else?
   B ☐ Oh, would you mind mailing these first-class letters?
   B ☐ Oh, would you mind getting me some first-class stamps?
   A ☐ No, not at all.
   A ☐ Not at all.

2. **C** ☐ May I help you?
   C ☐ Can I help you?
   A ☐ I'd like to have this package weighed.
   A ☐ I'd like to have you weigh this package.
   C ☐ Will there be anything else?
   C ☐ Do you need anything else?
   A ☐ No, thanks.
   A ☐ No, nothing else.

2 ▶ **Unscramble the words. Then match the words with the pictures.**

_b_ 1. gaswhin hamceni _washing machine_

___ 2. frumeep _____

___ 3. nacatrio _____

___ 4. cotrallcua _____

___ 5. iliveonset _____

___ 6. moptruce _____

___ 7. cavumu eelcran _____

___ 8. greatfreirro _____

___ 9. pumeka _____

___ 10. treeblac _____

Lesson 40

1 ► Andrew Barnes is running some errands. Listen to each conversation and write the number of the conversation on the picture that shows where it takes place.

2 ► Complete the sentences with appropriate verbs. Be sure to use the correct forms: infinitive, base form, past participle, etc.

1. If you happen ____*to go*____ by the bank, could you _____ this check _____?

2. I'd like to _____ you _____ this film.

3. While I'm here, I might as well _____ some laundry detergent.

4. Oh, you _____ to the coffee shop. Would you mind _____ me a hamburger and an order of french fries? I _____ get some money.

5. I really _____ I _____ the time to stop at the post office for you. I'm sorry.

6. I need _____ my hair _____. _____ you _____ of any good hairstylists around here?

Lesson 41

1 ▶ **Imagine you are on a TV game show. Listen to the announcer and follow his instructions.**

1. _____ *classroom* _____
2. _____
3. _____
4. _____
5. _____
6. _____
7. _____
8. _____
9. _____
10. _____
11. _____
12. _____

2 ▶ **Look again at the noun compounds you wrote in exercise 1. Make sure you spelled the words correctly. (Look in a dictionary if you're not sure.) Then underline the stressed syllable in each one.**

1. _____ *classroom* _____

3 ▶ **Sam and Beth Greene have decided to fix up their house. Who is going to do the work: the Greenes or someone else? Listen to the conversation and check (✔) the correct column.**

	The Greenes	Someone else
1. paint the outside of the house	✔	_____
2. paint the kitchen and dining room	_____	_____
3. wallpaper the bathrooms	_____	_____
4. shampoo the carpet	_____	_____
5. plant flowers and bushes outside	_____	_____
6. clean the garage	_____	_____
7. fix the roof	_____	_____
8. build a barbecue grill in the yard	_____	_____

Lesson 42

▶ **Read the letter. Then write a letter to the Wonder Electronics Company about your calculator that doesn't work.**

43 Center Avenue
Richmond, VA 23235

January 27, 1995

Spiffy Camera Company
546 Rosita Drive
Los Angeles, CA 90023

Dear Sir or Madam:

On December 13, I bought a Spiffy R82 camera. I have taken two rolls of film with the camera, but I believe that something is wrong with it. All of the photographs on both rolls had black lines on them.

I would like to have the camera repaired or replaced. I am sending the camera and a copy of the 60-day warranty with this letter.

Thank you for your attention.

Sincerely yours,

Jacobo Marciano

Jacobo Marciano

_____
_____
_____

Wonder Electronics Company
543 Circle Street
Chicago, IL 60626

_____ :

_____
_____
_____
_____
_____
_____
              _____

121447

Lesson 43

▶ **Complete the conversations with the sentences in the box.**

I can't talk very loudly. Someone's in my house.
He finished his work and came home early.
I had the most frightening experience last night.
I called the police. But while I was talking on the phone, he started coming up the stairs.
Why didn't you call?
Oh, Jerry. It's you!
Oh, no! He's coming upstairs.
Hello, I live at 41 Brookside …
You scared me to death. I thought you were coming home tomorrow.
At 41 Brookside Drive.
Well, I was reading in bed when I heard footsteps downstairs.
It was Jerry.

1. **A** Police.

   B *Hello, I live at 41 Brookside …* _____

   A Could you speak up, please?

   B _____

   A Where did you say you lived?

   B _____

   A Someone will be right there.

   B _____

   C Joanne?

   B _____

   C I'm sorry if I frightened you.

   B _____

   C Well, I got through a day early.

   B _____

   C I wanted to surprise you.

2. **B** _____

   D What happened?

   B _____

   D Oh, no! What did you do?

   B _____

   D You must have been terrified.

   B _____

   D Jerry? Isn't he out of town?

   B _____

Lesson 44

1 ▶ **Complete the conversations, using the information under the pictures. Tell what happened, using *while*.**

1. **A** <u>*While I was traveling across Death Valley, I ran out of gas.*</u>

   B What did you do?

   A _____

travel across Death Valley/run out of gas
wait for help

2. **A** _____
   _____
   _____

   B What did you do?

   A _____

drive to work/hit a tree
call the police

3. **A** _____
   _____
   _____

   B What did you do?

   A _____

wash the windows/fall off the ladder
ask my neighbor to call an ambulance

4. **A** _____
   _____
   _____

   B What did you do?

   A _____

swim in the ocean/see a shark
swim back to shore

2 ▶ **Complete the story with either the past continuous or the simple past tense of the verbs in parentheses.**

While I ___*was working*___ (work) late one night, I _____ (hear) a strange noise coming from the office next to mine. I _____ (think) all my coworkers were gone for the day, so the noise _____ (scare) me a little. I _____ (get up) to find out what it was when I _____ (hear) it again. I _____ (walk) to the door quickly and _____ (look) into the hallway. When I _____ (not, see) anything, I _____ (decide) to go into the office next door. While I _____ (turn) the doorknob, I _____ (hear) the noise again. I _____ (open) the door slowly and _____ (look) into the office. I couldn't see anything in the dark, so I _____ (turn on) the light. While my eyes _____ (get) used to the light, I _____ (hear) the noise again. It _____ (come) from behind the desk. While I _____ (walk) quietly toward the desk, I _____ (see) a pair of feet. My coworker Kathy _____ (sleep) on the floor behind her desk! Suddenly, she _____ (wake up) and _____ (see) me. "Oh, no!" she said. "Is it morning?"

   I _____ (laugh) very hard, so I _____ (not, answer) at first. Finally, while Kathy _____ (get up) off the floor, I _____ (stop) laughing.

   "I'm so embarrassed!" she said. "While I _____ (work) at my computer, I _____ (feel) really tired. I have to finish a report by tomorrow, so I _____ (decide) to take a nap. I guess I was more tired than I _____ (think)!"

3 ▶ **Listen to the conversations and write the numbers 1-3 on the correct pictures.**

Lesson 45

1 ▶ **Complete the conversations with negative yes-no questions.**

1. **A** *Isn't this your scarf?*

   B Yes, it is! It's my favorite scarf, too. Where did you find it?

2. **A** _____

   B No, I'm not. I have to go somewhere else that night.

   A That's too bad. Tony always gives really great parties.

3. **A** _____

   B Did you say *Fearless?* No, I haven't seen it. In fact, I've never heard of it.

4. **A** _____

   B No, she never learned how. Betsy's afraid of the water.

2 ▶ **Use the information to ask for and give reasons.**

1. Basketball wasn't much fun 100 years ago. After a player scored a point, someone had to climb a ladder to get the ball out of a peach basket.

   A *Why wasn't basketball much fun 100 years ago?*

   B *After a player scored a point, someone had to climb a ladder to get the ball out of a peach basket.*

2. Beethoven didn't hear his last musical works. He wrote them when he was completely deaf.

   A _____

   B _____

3. Franklin D. Roosevelt wasn't able to walk very well while he was President of the United States. He had polio several years before.

   A _____

   B _____

3 ▶ **Complete the conversations, using negative questions with *Why*.**

1. **A** Hello?

   B Hi, Bob. I just called your office. *Why aren't you at work?*

   A I have the flu.

2. **A** We had a good practice. Everybody was there except Pete.

   B _____

   A He had to go away on a business trip.

3. **A** It's late. _____

   B I can't. I have to stay up and finish this report.

4. **A** Kim and Lee have been to every state but Alaska and Hawaii.

   B _____

   A I don't know. They're too far away, I guess.

4 ▶ Imagine you run into Chris, someone you met at a party a few weeks ago. Chris asked you the questions in the box while you were at the party; however, he has a bad memory and now asks for the information again. Write Chris's questions and then answer them with your own information.

Where do you live?	When is your birthday?
How do you spell your last name?	Where were you born?
What do you do?	Who's your favorite singer?
Where are you studying English?	What's your phone number?

1. **Chris** *Where did you say you lived?* _____
   You _____

2. **Chris** _____
   You _____

3. **Chris** _____
   You _____

4. **Chris** _____
   You _____

5. **Chris** _____
   You _____

6. **Chris** _____
   You _____

7. **Chris** _____
   You _____

8. **Chris** _____
   You _____

5 ▶ Listen to each conversation and circle the correct words.

1. They (have, haven't) met before.

2. Her name is (Clara, Carla).

3. He has to go (out of town, downtown).

4. Her birthday is in (March, May).

5. He (likes, doesn't like) the food.

6. They bought a (two-bedroom, three-bedroom) house.

Lesson 46

1 ▶ **Read each sentence. Which action started first? Which action started next? Write *1* or *2* under each underlined verb form.**

1. I <u>was reading</u> in bed when I <u>heard</u> footsteps downstairs.
      1   *2*

2. I <u>heard</u> footsteps while I <u>was reading</u> in bed.
      ___   ___

3. While I <u>was driving</u> home, I <u>saw</u> a terrible accident on the highway.
          ___   ___

4. The phone <u>was ringing</u> when I <u>opened</u> the door.
             ___   ___

5. I <u>found</u> a wallet on the ground while I <u>was taking</u> a walk.
      ___   ___

6. When I <u>left</u> the house this morning, it <u>was pouring</u> rain.
          ___   ___

2 ▶ **Write an apology for each situation, using the ideas in the box.**

> Did I wake you up?   Did I scare you?
> Did my dog walk on your flowers?   Did I get you wet?

1. _I'm sorry if I scared you._____   2. _____

3. _____   4. _____

Lesson 47

1 ▶ **Listen and complete each conversation with *a*, *b*, or *c*.**

1. a. We went swimming.
   b. We were cooking dinner.
   c. We ran away.
2. a. A silver bracelet.
   b. January 3rd.
   c. Around 7:30.
3. a. She hates to write letters.
   b. No, not very often.
   c. Once or twice a month.

4. a. I was shopping for a new red sweater.
   b. I was looking for his mother.
   c. I took him to the manager.
5. a. You scared me to death.
   b. Yes, you are.
   c. As a matter of fact, I did.
6. a. Because I didn't have time.
   b. I did, but I ate them.
   c. O.K., I will.

2 ▶ **Listen to the questions and mark the intonation. Circle the arrow on the left (↗) when the speaker's voice goes up. Circle the arrow on the right (↘) when the speaker's voice goes down.**

1. ↗ ↘
2. ↗ ↘
3. ↗ ↘
4. ↗ ↘
5. ↗ ↘

6. ↗ ↘
7. ↗ ↘
8. ↗ ↘
9. ↗ ↘
10. ↗ ↘

3 ▶ **Listen to each part of the conversation between Jay and his friend Jill. Then answer the questions, using short answers wherever possible.**

Part 1

1. When did Jay have a frightening experience? *Last night.*_____
2. Where were Jay's parents? _____
3. Was Jay home alone? _____
4. What did Jay do for a couple of hours? _____
5. Why did Jay wake up suddenly? _____
6. Was Jay scared? _____

Part 2

7. Did Jay say anything when he heard the footsteps on the stairs? _____
8. Who opened the door to Jay's bedroom? _____
9. What did the person do in Jay's bedroom? _____
10. What did Jay do when the person left the house? _____

Lesson 48

▶ **Write an ending to this story.**

The House on the Hill

The house always scared me. When we were children, we used to play in the field across from it, but we never went near it. My parents told us not to. They said it was dangerous. We also heard about scary things that happened there at night. People talked about strange lights and sounds. So we stayed away.

One day while we were playing soccer, Theo kicked the ball into the yard of the house. All of us were afraid to go after it, so we decided to draw straws. The one who got the short straw had to go get the ball.

I drew the short straw. I had to go.

I didn't want to seem afraid, but I was scared to death. I walked slowly through the gate. I thought the ball was just over the old fence, but I couldn't find it. While I was looking, I saw footprints. They led from the place where I thought the ball was to the front door of the house. I almost ran back across the street, but I didn't want the other kids to know I was afraid.

"I'll just go and see if someone in the house has our ball," I thought. I took a deep breath and went to the door. Just before I started to knock, the door opened.

_____

_____

_____

_____

_____

_____

_____

_____

_____

_____

_____

_____

Review of units 5–7

1 ▶ **Write an appropriate response to each sentence.**

1. **A** I'm sorry if I scared you.
   B *Oh, that's O.K. Don't worry about it.* _____

2. **A** Haven't we met somewhere before?
   B _____

3. **A** Would you mind closing that window?
   B _____

4. **A** If I had more time, I'd travel.
   B _____

5. **A** I was born in Florida, but I grew up in New Jersey.
   B _____

6. **A** We had a great time on our trip, but someone broke into our house while
   we were away.
   B _____

7. **A** Now, what was I saying?
   B _____

8. **A** Why haven't you gotten a haircut this month?
   B _____

9. **A** Can I get you anything while I'm out?
   B _____

10. **A** If you happen to go by a post office, would you mind mailing this package?
    B _____

11. **A** I sprained my ankle while I was jogging in the park.
    B _____

12. **A** Where did you say you were from?
    B _____

2 ▶ **Rewrite the sentences, using the causative.**

1. I'd like you to develop this film.
   I'd like to have this film developed.

2. I'd like you to make two copies of each picture.
   _____

3. I'd also like you to repair my camera.
   _____

4. I want someone to deliver the pictures and camera to my office.
   _____

5. I'd like you to do the work as quickly as possible.
   _____

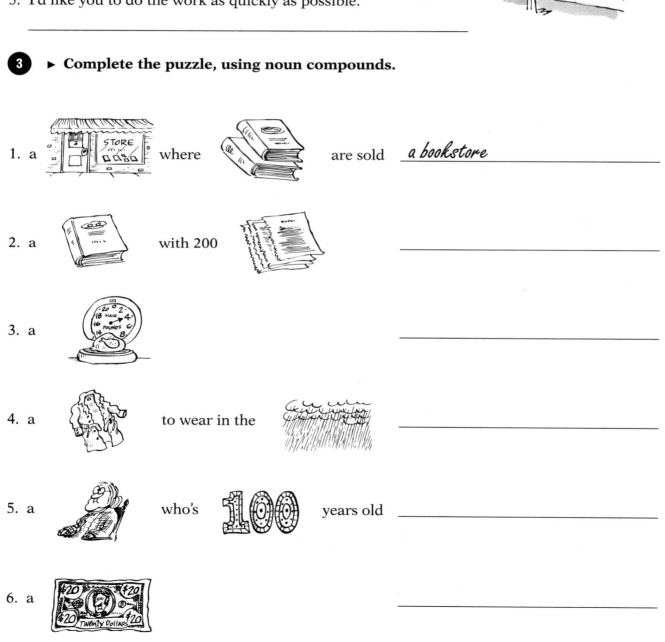

3 ▶ **Complete the puzzle, using noun compounds.**

1. a [store] where [books] are sold   *a bookstore*

2. a [book] with 200 [pages]   _____

3. a [scale] _____

4. a [coat] to wear in the [rain]   _____

5. a [man] who's [100] years old   _____

6. a [twenty dollars]   _____

Lesson 49

▶ **Complete the conversations with the sentences in the box.**

Oh, I'd really appreciate it.	I really wish I could go, but I have too much work to do.
Hmm…What time are we supposed to meet them?	Oh, am I supposed to call her back?
I'm sorry to let you down, but my job is on the line.	You'd better not count on me for that, either.
Not at all. Go right ahead. Sonia, I really appreciate your staying late.	That's O.K. I understand.
	We were planning to go to a play, but now I have this report to write.

1. **A** Carlos, your wife just called.
   B *Oh, am I supposed to call her back?*
   A No, she'll call back later.
   B _____
   _____
   A Is there anything I can do to give you a hand?
   B _____
   A It's no problem.

2. **C** Hi, Carlos. It's me. Listen, Sandra and Ray would like to have dinner with us before the play.
   B _____
   C At about six.
   B _____
   _____
   C Oh, that's too bad. What about the play?
   B _____
   C Oh, Carlos, not again!
   B _____
   _____
   C O.K., O.K. I'm sorry if I sounded annoyed with you.
   B _____

3. **A** I'm just about finished. …Uh, would you mind if I opened a window? It's getting stuffy in here.
   B _____
   _____
   A Oh, I'm happy to help you. I'm sure you'd do the same for me.

Lesson 50

1 ► Peggy Barnes had such a busy week at her restaurant that she had to cancel most of her plans. Read the notes she made on her calendar. Then complete Peggy's conversations.

Sunday 1	Monday 2	Tuesday 3	Wednesday 4	Thursday 5	Friday 6
dinner w/ Mom & Dad 6:00	concert w/ Carmen 8:00	jogging w/ Chris - 7:00 A.M.	lunch w/ Amy - 12:00	swimming w/ Mom - 4:30	jogging w/ Chris - 7:00
ballet w/ Jim - 8:30	write the week's menus	see some food suppliers 7:30 A.M.	do the breakfast dishes	go over the new accounts and pay the bills	basketball game - 9:00 P.M.

1. **Peggy**   Carmen, I'm sorry to let you down, but I can't go _____to the concert tonight_____.
   I have _____the week's menus to write_____.

   Carmen   I'm sorry, too, Peggy, but I understand how it is.

2. **Peggy**   Hello, Chris? Are you awake? I'm sorry to call so early, but I thought you'd be up.
   Look, I won't be able to go _____.
   I have _____.

   Chris   Oh, that's O.K., Peggy. I'll just go back to bed. See you on Friday.

3. **Peggy**   Amy, I can't go _____.
   I wish I could, but the dishwasher broke last night. I have

   _____.

   Amy   Why don't I come over and give you a hand?
   Peggy   Would you? Amy, you're a real friend.

4. **Peggy**   Sorry, Mom, but I can't go _____.
   I have _____.

   Mother   That's all right, dear. We'll try for next week.

2 ► Listen to the conversations and write the numbers 1-6 on the correct pictures.

3 ▶ Complete the conversations with advice using *had better* (*not*). Use the ideas in the box.

Turn it down.	Talk to her about it.
Don't go out.	Don't try.
Don't drink it.	Don't put it off too long.
Get him something special.	Take him to the doctor.

1. **A** I'm a little worried about Lisa. She's been late every day this week.

   B *You'd better talk to her about it.* _____

2. **A** It's kind of late. I hope my music isn't bothering the neighbors.

   B _____

3. **A** I heard on the radio that there's going to be a big storm tonight.

   B _____

4. **A** The baby has been coughing since yesterday morning.

   B _____

5. **A** I heard this morning that the concert tickets are almost sold out, and I haven't gotten

   mine yet.

   B _____

6. **A** This milk smells a little funny, doesn't it?

   B _____

7. **A** Tomorrow is our twentieth wedding anniversary. What should I give my husband?

   B _____

8. **A** This luggage is so heavy that I'm not sure I can carry it all.

   B _____

4 ▶ Look at the pictures and write sentences asking permission.

1. It's getting chilly in here.

Would you mind if I closed the window?

2. I'm having a hard time concentrating.

3. It's really warm in here.

Lesson 51

1 ▶ Imagine that the people in the picture are talking to you.
Write the conversations, responding with your own information.

Could you help me paint my kitchen next Sunday?

Could you help me fix my car tonight?

Could you help me with my homework Saturday afternoon?

Could you help me write a letter to my landlord tomorrow morning?

Could you help me pick out my wedding dress on Saturday morning?

1. **A** *I'd really appreciate it if you could help me paint my kitchen next Sunday.*

   B *I think I can. I'm supposed to go camping, but I should be able to change my plans. I wish I could, but I have to work that day.*

2. **A** _____

   B _____

3. **A** _____

   B _____

4. **A** _____

   B _____

5. **A** _____

   B _____

2 ▶ Listen to each sentence and decide if the speaker is asking a favor or saying thank you. Check (✔) the correct column.

	ASKING A FAVOR	SAYING THANK YOU
1.	_____	✔
2.	_____	_____
3.	_____	_____
4.	_____	_____
5.	_____	_____
6.	_____	_____

Lesson 52

1 ▶ **Terry is asking Donna about their plans for dinner with Ted Duncan, a business associate of theirs. Write Terry's questions using *be supposed to*.**

Terry   *When are we supposed to have dinner with Ted?* Is it Friday or Saturday?

Donna   Friday.

Terry   _____

Donna   At the restaurant. It's the Garden of Delight on Maple Avenue.

Terry   _____

Donna   No, don't bring anything. We're just going to discuss plans for the new office.

Terry   Oh, I forgot to ask you … _____

Donna   At seven o'clock. But you know Ted. He's always a little late.

2 ▶ **Glenn is planning to move this Sunday, and he's asking some of his friends to help. Write Glenn's requests. Then write his friends' responses, using a form of *have to* or *be supposed to*.**

1. Chuck is going out of town this weekend, and he can't change his plans.

   Glenn   *I'd really appreciate it if you could help me move on Sunday.*

   Chuck   *I wish I could, but I have to go out of town.*
   I'm sorry to let you down.

   Glenn   That's O.K. Thanks anyway.

   > Maybe he could help me move on Sunday.

2. Zuber's boss has asked him to work all day Saturday.

   Zuber   I hear you have a new apartment. When are you supposed to move?

   Glenn   This Sunday. By the way,

   _____

   Zuber   _____

   You'd better not count on me. I'll probably be at the office until the evening.

   Glenn   That's O.K. I understand.

   > Maybe he could help me get some big boxes on Saturday.

3. Mary Ellen's sister wants her to baby-sit, but maybe her brother can do it.

   Glenn   Mary Ellen, _____

   _____

   Mary Ellen   _____

   > Maybe she could help me pack Saturday night.

   Glenn   Do you think so? That would be great.

Lesson 53

1 ▶ Here are some notes that two coworkers wrote to each other. Complete the notes with appropriate words.

MEMO

Jane,

I came by your desk _while_ you were out. Did you _____ the notes from yesterday's meeting? _____ the way, I can't go _____ lunch. I have the monthly report _____ do, and I'm supposed _____ finish it today. Sorry to _____ you down.

Michael

MEMO

Michael,

We keep missing each other. _____ are the notes you asked _____. You're right--you'd _____ finish that monthly report. Ms. Williams was _____ about it earlier. She said _____ it's late one more time, _____ going to find someone else _____ do it. How about having dinner _____ celebrate your finishing the report?

Jane

MEMO

Jane,

I don't think I can go _____ dinner, unless you'd like _____ midnight snack. I'm having trouble _____ the report, and I may _____ here all night.

Michael

MEMO

Michael,

_____ there anything I can do _____ help you?

Jane

---

2 ▶ Now answer the questions about the memos in exercise 1.

1. What is Michael supposed to do today? _Finish the monthly report._
2. Did Michael and Jane already have plans for lunch? _____
3. What does Michael want Jane to give him? _____
4. When Jane went to give Michael the notes, was he at his desk? _____
5. What advice does Jane give Michael? _____
6. If Michael doesn't finish the report on time, what will happen? _____
   _____
7. Why can't Michael go to dinner? _____
8. What does Jane offer to do? _____

Lesson 54

1 ▶ Listen to each conversation and decide what Brad Jensen is doing. Check (✔) the correct column.

	canceling plans	asking permission	asking about an obligation	saying thank you	giving advice
Conversation 1					✔
Conversation 2					
Conversation 3					
Conversation 4					
Conversation 5					

2 ▶ Listen again to each conversation in exercise 1. Then write *That's right* or *That's wrong*.

1. Brad thinks Ms. Swift will be angry if she's interrupted. <u>*That's right.*</u>

2. Brad didn't remember the meeting until Judy reminded him of it. _____

3. Ms. Swift doesn't mind if Brad hands the report in late. _____

4. Brad didn't have any plans for tonight. _____

5. Judy can probably change her plans. _____

3 ▶ Listen to each conversation. Circle *Yes* if the picture is correct. Circle *No* if it is not correct.

1. Yes   (No)

2. Yes   No

3. Yes   No

4. Yes   No

Lesson 55

► **Read the memo. Then write a reply to it. Thank Mr. Ortiz for asking you to speak at the meeting and say that you are able to attend the meeting but you're not sure what he wants you to do. Ask him any questions you may have.**

Acme Computer Company
333 Fifth Avenue, New York, NY 10022
MEMO

DATE: January 10

SUBJECT: Invitation to speak at the sales meeting

TO: _____

FROM: Phil Ortiz

Can you attend the sales meeting next Thursday, January 19, at 10:00 A.M.? I'd really appreciate it if you would talk about the new computer game you've been working on.

Acme Computer Company
333 Fifth Avenue, New York, NY 10022
MEMO

TO: _____   DATE: _____

FROM: _____   SUBJECT: _____
_____

_____

_____

_____

_____

_____

Lesson 56

▶ **Put the lines of the conversations in order. Then write the conversations.**

1. ____ That's right. I asked them not to call me unless it's absolutely necessary.

____ Maybe I'll clean out the attic.

____ I just don't want you to have any more back trouble.

_1_ You know, this is the first Saturday I've had off in months.

____ Now who's the doctor, you or me?

____ Well, what are you planning to do with all this free time?

____ Well, remember, you're not supposed to lift anything heavy.

____ You mean you don't have to go to the hospital at all?

A *You know, this is the first Saturday I've had off in months.* _____

B _____

A _____

B _____

A _____

B _____

A _____

B _____

2. ____ What about me? Do I have to go?

____ Hey, don't forget . . . we're invited to the Scotts' for dinner tonight.

____ At about seven.

____ Not if you don't want to.

____ What time are we supposed to be there?

B _____

A _____

B _____

C _____

A _____

Lesson 57

1 ▶ **Match the two parts of each sentence. Then write the sentences.**

1. We won't have anything to cook for dinner
2. I won't be late for work
3. I'll cook you your favorite dinner
4. We'll fail the exam
5. We'll do well in our English course
6. I'll miss my flight

a. unless I leave right now.
b. if we don't go to the supermarket.
c. if you drive me to the supermarket.
d. if we study hard.
e. unless we memorize these verbs.
f. if I leave right now.

1. _We won't have anything to cook for dinner if we don't go to the supermarket._
2. _____
   _____
3. _____
   _____
4. _____
   _____
5. _____
   _____
6. _____
   _____

2 ▶ **Read the rules for the Brookville public swimming pool. Then complete the conversation with *if* or *unless*.**

1. **A** Is the pool open on Mondays?
   B It's closed ___*unless*___ it's a holiday.

2. **A** Can I bring in something to drink?
   B You can _____ it's in a glass container.
   It's O.K. _____ it's in a plastic container.

3. **A** A friend is supposed to meet me here at 7:30 Saturday evening. Will the pool still be open?
   B Not _____ the sun has gone down.

4. **A** Is it O.K. if my eight-year-old nephew swims here?
   B Not _____ an adult is with him.

5. **A** Can we play water volleyball here?
   B Not _____ the game is supervised.

6. **A** Do we have to wear bathing caps?
   B You do _____ you have long hair.

POOL HOURS: TUES. – FRI. 12:00 — 6:00 PM
SAT. & SUN. 10:00 TO DARK
CLOSED MONDAYS EXCEPT HOLIDAYS

SWIMMING ALLOWED ONLY
IF LIFEGUARD IS PRESENT.

FOOD AND DRINKS ALLOWED
IF IN PLASTIC CONTAINERS.

NOT ALLOWED:
1. RUNNING OR ROUGH PLAY EXCEPT SUPERVISED WATER SPORTS
2. CHILDREN UNDER 12 UNLESS ACCOMPANIED BY AN ADULT
3. SWIMMERS WITH LONG HAIR UNLESS BATHING CAPS ARE WORN
4. DOGS, CATS, OR OTHER ANIMALS
5. GLASS CONTAINERS

3 ▶ **All the sentences below are correct. Listen to each conversation and decide which sentence you hear. Circle *a* or *b*.**

1. a. Yes, if it stops raining.
   b. (Not unless it stops raining.)

2. a. Well, don't go if you don't want to.
   b. Well, don't go unless you want to.

3. a. She won't be able to go unless she can find a baby-sitter.
   b. She'll be able to go if she can find a baby-sitter.

4. a. Yes, if there's something good on.
   b. Not unless there's something good on.

5. a. You'll make it if you leave right now.
   b. You won't make it unless you leave right now.

6. a. Not if it doesn't snow.
   b. Not unless it snows.

4 ▶ **Look again at the rules in exercise 2. Then complete the lifeguard's explanations with affirmative and negative forms of *be supposed to*.**

1. O.K., everybody out of the pool! You *aren't supposed to* _____ swim after dark.

2. You'll have to take that outside. You _____ put all drinks in plastic containers.

3. You _____ have your dog in here at any time. Either he has to leave or you both do.

4. You're ten? You _____ swim here unless an adult is with you.

5. You have long hair. You _____ wear a bathing cap.

5 ▶ **Complete each conversation with a negative form of *be supposed to* or *have to*.**

1. **A** Would you like some strawberries?
   B No, thank you. I *'m not supposed to* _____ eat strawberries. I'm allergic to them.

2. **A** You _____ smoke in here.
   B Oh, I'm sorry. I didn't see the sign.

3. **A** How's Emily? Is she feeling better?
   B Yes, but she _____ go back to work yet. The doctor told her to stay in bed for another week.

4. **A** Isn't Toshi going to take another English course?
   B No. He did so well on the final exam that he _____.

5. **A** I don't want any vegetables, Mom.
   B All right. You _____ take any. But remember the rule: Unless you eat your vegetables, you can't have any dessert.

Lesson 58

▶ **American football is a rough sport. During a recent game, five members of the Riverview Rams were injured. Imagine that you are speaking to each of the players. Write five conversations. Use the words in the box to describe the injuries. Then give an appropriate response. (Several different answers are possible.)**

bruise	break
ankle	knee
sprain	pull
finger	muscle
cut	back

1. **A** _Did you hurt yourself?_
   B _Yes, I think I sprained my knee._
   A _You'd better put some ice on it._

2. **A** _____
   B _____
   A _____

3. **A** _____
   B _____
   A _____

4. **A** _____
   B _____
   A _____

5. **A** _____
   B _____
   A _____

Lesson 59

1 ► In each conversation, change the second sentence to a reported request or instruction.

1. **A** What did the doctor tell you?

   B "Stay off your foot for a few days."

   He told me to stay off my foot for a few days.

2. **A** What did Marisa say?

   B "Don't come until eight o'clock."

   _____

3. **A** What did Adam ask you just now?

   B "Don't tell anyone the news."

   _____

4. **A** What do the washing instructions say?

   B "Don't wash the shirt in hot water."

   _____

5. **A** What did your mother tell your brother before he left?

   B "Call me after your game."

   _____

6. **A** What did the letter carrier tell you this morning? He looked angry.

   B "Keep your dog in the house when I'm on your street."

   _____

2 ► Listen to each conversation and circle *a* or *b*.

1. She said _____ the plants every day.
   a. to water
   b. not to water

2. She told him _____ his hands in the bathroom.
   a. to wash
   b. not to wash

3. He told her _____ all the exercises.
   a. not to do
   b. to do

4. He asked them _____ at the airport.
   a. to pick him up
   b. not to pick him up

5. The label on the blanket says _____ it in cold water.
   a. to wash
   b. not to wash

6. He _____ the meeting.
   a. said she shouldn't come to
   b. didn't say anything about

Lesson 60

1 ▶ **Listen to each conversation and choose the picture that matches. Circle _a_ or _b_.**

1. (a.)   b.

2. a.   b.

3. a.   b.

4. a.   b.

2 ▶ **Answer the questions with your own information. Use complete sentences.**

1. Think about your home. List two things you aren't supposed to do at home and two things you don't have to do. Follow the examples.
   I'm not supposed to use too much water.
   I don't have to do my own laundry.

   1. _____
   2. _____
   3. _____
   4. _____

2. Think about your childhood. List two things that adults asked/told you to do when you were a child and two things they asked/told you not to do. Follow the examples.
   My mother asked me to wash my hands before dinner.
   My sixth-grade teacher told me not to talk to my friends during class.

   1. _____
   2. _____
   3. _____
   4. _____

Lesson 61

📼 **1** ▶ **Listen and complete each conversation with the most logical response.**
Circle *a* or *b*.

1. a. Yes, if there's snow.
   b. Yes, unless there's snow.

2. a. Yes, unless I don't finish this report by five.
   b. Yes, unless I finish this report by five.

3. a. Oh, I'm really disappointed that he has to work.
   b. Oh, I'm so glad he doesn't have to go to work.

4. a. I hope we won't have to wait too long.
   b. I'm surprised she doesn't want us to wait.

5. a. I'm not? Then I guess I'll go home.
   b. I don't? Then I think I'll go to a movie.

6. a. Yes, if I'm not in a meeting.
   b. Yes, unless I'm not in a meeting.

2 ▶ **Listen to the conversations and mark the strongest vowels or**
vowel combinations in the sentences. In some sentences, you
will mark two strongly stressed vowels.

1. **A** You aren't going to eat that, are you?

   B Well, yes, I am. It looks delicious.

   A But you aren't supposed to eat spicy foods.

   B Oh, I know. I'm just going to have a little.

2. **A** Are we still going camping this weekend?

   B We won't be able to go unless this weather gets better.

   A Well, I don't really feel like going anyway.

   B Really? Well, you don't have to go unless you want to.

Lesson 62

▶ **You and a friend are going to a dinner party at the Gatsbys', but you don't know how to get there. Your friend calls another friend to ask for directions. Read the conversation. Then write the directions below.**

A Hello?

B Hi. Listen, do you know how to get to the Gatsbys'?

A Yes. I just got directions from Mr. Gatsby. Let's see. … First, he told me to go north on Hanes Road and to turn right on Smith Boulevard. He said to go about five blocks on Smith. He told me not to turn left on Newton but to keep to the right on Smith. After five blocks, there are five streets that come together. Mr. Gatsby told me to turn right at the second street—that's Cherry Lane—and to follow Cherry almost to the end. Their house is the last one on the left: 214 Cherry Lane.

B That doesn't sound too hard. Thanks a lot.

A You're welcome. See you at the Gatsbys'.

Go north on Hanes Road and

UNIT 10 • LESSONS 63 – 68

Lesson 63

▶ **Read each conversation. Then complete the summary.**

1. **Mr. Dell**   What do you think this is, a social hour?
   Maybe if you two did less talking,
   you'd get more work done.

   Tanya   Don't take it personally. Mr. Dell hasn't been
   himself lately.

   Harold   That's for sure.

   Erica   He's been in a bad mood for weeks.

   Mr. Dell _gets angry_ at Harold and Erica for no real reason. He says
   that they _____ if they did less talking. Tanya tells Harold and
   Erica _____, because Mr. Dell _____
   lately. Harold agrees, and Erica thinks Mr. Dell _____ for weeks.

2. **Tanya**   Don, maybe it's none of my business, but ... well, you haven't been yourself lately.
   I mean, you've been losing your temper over nothing.

   Don   I know. I shouldn't have blown up like that. I don't know what came over me. And
   it's not just here. I've been getting into arguments with Donna and yelling at the
   kids ...

   Tanya   Have you been doing anything besides working?

   Don   Not really. I haven't been getting much sleep either.
   But what can I do? I've got to get this work done.

   Tanya   Well, you'd better not push yourself too hard, or
   you'll get sick. Then you won't be able to get
   anything done.

   Tanya goes into Don's office because she wants to _____.
   Tanya starts the conversation by saying, " _____, but ... ." She tells Don
   that _____ himself lately and that he's been losing
   _____. Don knows he shouldn't have blown up
   _____. He says that he's been _____ his
   wife and _____ his children. When Tanya asks Don if he has been
   doing _____, he answers, " _____." Then he
   says he hasn't been getting _____. Tanya gives Don a warning: "Well,
   you'd better not _____, or you'll _____."

Lesson 64

1 ▶ **Complete the conversations by giving advice.**

1. **A** I've been having trouble getting to sleep at night.
   B *If I were you, I wouldn't drink so much coffee.*

2. **A** I haven't been doing very well in English class lately.
   B _____

3. **A** My back's been giving me a lot of trouble again.
   B _____

4. **A** I've been gaining a lot of weight.
   B _____

2 ▶ **Complete the conversations, using a form of the present perfect continuous.**

1. **A** *Have you been getting enough exercise?*
   B No, I haven't. I really should take up a sport.

2. **A** _____
   B No. I lie awake every night for hours, and then when I finally fall asleep, it's almost time to get up.

3. **A** _____
   B No. I really should eat three meals a day.

4. **A** _____
   B I can't help it. I'm just in a bad mood all the time.

5. **A** _____
   B Much better, thanks. My allergies don't bother me much during the winter.

3 ▶ **Listen to each problem and choose the best advice from the list.**

1. ___e___
2. _____
3. _____
4. _____
5. _____
6. _____
7. _____
8. _____

a. If I were you, I'd go lie down for a while.
b. If I were you, I'd take it to a good mechanic.
c. I wouldn't drink it if I were you.
d. If I were you, I'd go see a doctor.
e. I'd take some time off if I were you.
f. If I were you, I wouldn't let them use it.
g. I'd stay home tonight if I were you.
h. If I were you, I'd take it out of the oven now.

4 ► **Willy Brown graduated from college a few years ago. As class secretary, it's his job to find out what his classmates have been doing and to write class notes about them for the *Alumni News*. Read Willy's notes. Then complete the sentences with a form of the present perfect continuous.**

Jack Riley Jr. is living in New York and going to law school at New York University. He made both changes in September. On weekends, he sails his boat up the Hudson River. They say law school isn't easy, but sailing the Hudson?? Jack sure knows how to take care of himself. . . . **Donna (Jennings) Eskar** started teaching at a community college in Winfield, New Hampshire last fall. She's teaching English and French. Donna and her husband, Arnie, live at Lake Winfield. They moved there after their wedding in July. Best wishes, Donna! . . . **Paul Wilson** hasn't been so lucky. He lost his job and is looking for another one. Paul pulled a muscle in his leg—nothing serious, but he had to quit playing tennis. He took up golf, though, and plays regularly. Maybe that's why he doesn't have another job yet? (Sorry, Paul. I know you're trying to find one. Good luck.). . . **Debbie Leone** is traveling around the world! I talked with Debbie's mother, who says that Debbie quit her job three months ago and took off. She was last heard from in Kashmir, where she was visiting friends who live on a houseboat. No one has to tell Debbie to slow down. . . . **Gail Farmer** is living in San Francisco and taking care of three-year-old twins. Not hers! She works as a nanny for a young couple. Gail's been in San Francisco for almost a year now and enjoys the life there very much. It's a big change from Allaway, Nebraska.

1. Jack Riley Jr. *has been going* _____ to law school.

2. Donna Eskar _____ at a community college since last fall.

3. Donna and Arnie _____ at Lake Winfield since July.

4. Paul Wilson _____ tennis, but he _____
   a lot of golf. He _____ a job too.

5. Debbie Leone _____ around the world.

6. Gail Farmer _____ in San Francisco for almost a year. She
   _____ three-year-old twins.

5 ► **These are parts of the conversations Willy had when he was trying to find out about his classmates' activities. Use the information in the class notes to complete the conversations with information questions in the present perfect continuous.**

1. **Willy** *What have you been doing lately?* _____
   Jack Well, I moved to New York and started studying law.

2. **Willy** _____
   Jack At New York University.

3. **Willy** _____
   Donna Since we got married in July.

4. **Willy** _____
   Paul I pulled a muscle in my leg.

5. **Willy** _____
   Mrs. Leone Traveling around the world.

Lesson 65

1 ▶ **Describe each person's feelings.**

1. *He's in a bad mood. He feels like running away.*

2. _____

3. _____

4. _____

5. _____
   _____

2 ▶ **Complete the conversations with reflexive pronouns.**

1. **A** How did Diana cut ____*herself*____?
   B I don't know _____. She won't tell me.

2. **A** Jackie, I don't think you've been taking very good care of _____.
   B It's just that the twins take up all of my time. I really don't have a minute to think of _____. I'll be glad when they can do some things for _____.

3. **A** Did you and Bob enjoy _____ in Greece?
   B It was a wonderful trip, but we spent too much money on _____. I bought _____ an expensive necklace, and Bob bought _____ a painting.
   A Ray and I have done that kind of thing _____.

4. **A** You know, I'm a little worried about Jenny. She's hasn't been _____ lately, and she's been spending a lot of time by _____.
   B I wouldn't worry too much if I were you. Most teenagers like being by _____ once in a while. I bet you were just like Jenny when you were fourteen _____.

3 ▶ **Give warnings to the people in the pictures.**

1. _You'd better not drink any more coffee,_
or you'll have trouble sleeping tonight.

2. _____
   _____

3. _____
   _____

4. _____
   _____

4 ▶ **Answer the questions with your own information.**

1. What do you feel like doing when you're in a good mood?

   _____

   _____

2. What do you feel like doing when you're in a bad mood?

   _____

   _____

3. Do you enjoy doing things by yourself, or do you enjoy yourself more with other people?

   _____

4. What was the last thing you bought yourself?

   _____

5. What advice would you give a friend who hasn't been taking care of himself/herself?

   _____

6. What's the word in English for people who think only of themselves? (Use a dictionary
   if necessary.)

   _____

Lesson 66

1 ▶ **Rewrite the sentences, using reflexive pronouns.**

1. We've felt like that, too.
   We've felt like that ourselves.

2. He's been acting strange lately.

   _____

3. Did you do your homework without help, or did someone help you?

   _____

   _____

4. We haven't been eating right or getting enough rest.

   _____

5. They had a lot of fun at the party last night.

   _____

6. She isn't allowed to go to the mall alone.

   _____

7. Were you hurt when you fell off your bike?

   _____

2 ▶ **Complete the conversation with appropriate words from the box.
(You won't use all the words, and you might use some words more than once.)**

at	of	over
away	off	to
for	on	under
in	out	up

A I'm very sorry that I blew ____up____ like that. I shouldn't have lost my temper _____ such a small thing.

B Thanks _____ apologizing, but it isn't necessary. We're all _____ a bad mood sometimes. I often feel like yelling _____ somebody.

A Well, I'm sorry it was you that I screamed _____. I wonder what came _____ me. I don't *feel* that I'm _____ a lot of pressure, but maybe I am. I haven't been sleeping very well lately.

B You can tell me it's none _____ my business, but I don't think you realize how hard you've been working. Maybe if you took some time _____ and got _____ for a while, you'd feel better.

A I could use a vacation—that's _____ sure!

Lesson 67

1 ▶ Mrs. Barnes drops in at Peggy's restaurant, the Garden of Delight. Listen to the three parts of the conversation between Peggy and her mother. Then answer the questions with short answers.

Part 1

1. Have Peggy and her mother been getting together a lot lately?
   No, they haven't.

2. Has Peggy been busy at the restaurant?

3. Does Peggy want her mother's help with the flowers?

Part 2

4. Has Peggy been herself the last few weeks?

5. Has Peggy found a dishwasher yet?

Part 3

6. Does Peggy sometimes feel like quitting?

7. Has Mrs. Barnes ever felt like Peggy?

2 ▶ Listen again to the three parts of the conversation. Then write *That's right* or *That's wrong* after each statement.

1. Peggy hasn't had much time for herself. *That's right.*
2. Peggy's mother doesn't offer to help her. _____
3. Peggy's been losing her temper a lot. _____
4. Peggy hasn't been getting enough sleep. _____
5. Peggy hasn't been exercising enough. _____
6. Peggy's been pushing herself too hard. _____
7. Peggy's mother doesn't understand how she's feeling. _____

3 ▶ Listen to each question and complete the answer.

1. Yes, *he has.* _____
2. Yes, _____
3. No, _____
4. Yes, _____

5. No, _____
6. No, _____
7. Yes, _____
8. No, _____

Lesson 68

▶ **Write a letter to Dr. Harris about a problem that you or someone you know has been having.**

THE DOCTOR IS IN ─────────
by Dr. Bernard Harris

Dear Dr. Harris:

    I've been working very hard lately, and I've been having a lot of trouble sleeping. I often wake up in the middle of the night and worry about my problems at work. I used to enjoy playing tennis, but lately I haven't been playing at all. At times, I'm really in a bad mood. People have been telling me that I'm working too hard, but I have so much to do. What can I do?

Sleepless

Dear Sleepless:

    You've been pushing yourself too hard. You need to find ways to relax, and exercise can help. If I were you, I'd start playing tennis again. You should also try to take some time off from work. I know this may be difficult, but you'll feel better and probably find work easier when you return. If you continue to have trouble sleeping, be sure to see your doctor.

_____:

_____

_____

_____

_____

_____

_____

_____

_____

                                      _____

Lesson 69

▶ **Complete the conversation with the sentences in the box.**

> Hey, this sounds serious!
> I haven't been playing at all lately. I've just had too much work.
> Well, things should calm down pretty soon.
> Rachel! How have you been?
> I like it a lot, but I've worked every weekend for the last few months.
> I haven't been going.
> I've been meaning to call you. What have you been doing lately?
> Well, if I had more time and if I weren't so stressed out, I'd go.
> If I have time next week, why don't we play tennis together?
> I've been doing construction work.

A *Rachel! How have you been?* _____

B Fine, Marty. Say, where have you been keeping yourself? I haven't seen you at the gym in ages.

A _____

B I've missed you.

A _____

B You *do* look tired.

A _____

B Well, I've been playing a lot of tennis. I've even signed up for lessons.

A _____

B Well, I've always wanted to play tennis better. I've already played three nights this week.

A _____

B How come you've been working so hard?

A _____

B That's great. Do you like it?

A _____
_____

B Gee, I don't know how you do it!

A _____

B I hope so.

A _____

B Let's do that. Give me a call, and we can set up a time.

Lesson 70

1 ► Imagine you are talking to the people in the pictures. Write four conversations.

1. **A** <u>What have you been doing lately?</u>
   B <u>I've been trying to get better at tennis.</u>
   A <u>Oh, really?</u>
   B <u>Yes. In fact, I'e played four times this week.</u>

2. **A** _____
   B _____
   A _____
   B _____

3. **A** _____
   B _____
   A _____
   B _____

4. **A** _____
   B _____
   A _____
   B _____

2 ▸ Complete the conversations with either a present perfect or a present perfect continuous form of the verbs in the box. (You may use some verbs more than once.)

be	find	have	see	try
do	finish	read	travel	work

1. **A** I _haven't seen_____ Alfonso in ages. What _____ he

   _____?

   B He _____ away for the last two weeks. He _____ for his

   company.

   A I thought he was looking for a new job. _____ he _____ one

   yet?

   B Not yet, but he _____.

2. **A** _____ you _____ any good books lately?

   B I _____ Stephen King's new book. I _____ it yet, though. It's

   over 800 pages long. How about you?

   A I'm sorry to say that I _____ anything except the newspaper in weeks. I

   just _____ a chance. I _____ day and night.

3 ▸ Listen to each conversation. Then complete each sentence. Circle *a* or *b*.

1. He _____ been working hard.
   a. has
   b.) hasn't

2. She _____ finished painting her living room.
   a. has
   b. hasn't

3. She hasn't called him because she _____.
   a. hasn't had a chance
   b. hasn't been feeling well

4. He _____ for 20 years.
   a. taught
   b. has been teaching

5. The Delgados _____ lived there for years.
   a. have
   b. haven't

6. They haven't seen each other in _____.
   a. months
   b. years

4 ▸ Imagine someone suggests these plans. Write responses without making firm plans, using your own information.

1. I'm thinking of going shopping on Saturday. Do you want to join me?

   _____

2. How about going out for dinner one day next week?

   _____

3. Do you want to go jogging sometime?

   _____

Lesson 71

1 ► **Match the two parts of each sentence.**

___d___ 1. If I'm too tired,

_____ 2. If I'm not too tired,

_____ 3. If I were too tired,

_____ 4. If I weren't so tired,

a. I wouldn't go dancing.

b. I'll go dancing.

c. I'd go dancing.

d. I won't go dancing.

2 ► **Look at Gary's and Jennifer's calendars for this week and write who says each statement.**

Gary's calendar

Mon	Tues	Wed	Thurs
1	2	3	4
call about Tennis class	gym	work late	gym?

Jennifer's calendar

Mon	Tues	Wed	Thurs
1	2	3	4
work late	~~gym~~ work late	work late	~~gym~~ work late

1. "If I had more time, I'd go to the gym." _Jennifer_____

2. "If I have some time on Thursday, I'll go to the gym." _____

3. "I haven't been getting any exercise lately." _____

4. "I'm thinking about taking tennis lessons." _____

5. "If I weren't working late, I'd go to the gym." _____

3 ► **Listen to the conversations and circle the correct words.**

1. The woman tells the man (not to study so much, (to study more)).

2. The Baileys' lights are (on, off).

3. The woman (has, hasn't) written to her friend Roberta.

4. The man (may, is going to) paint the bedroom this weekend.

5. It (isn't, may be) too late to buy tickets for the football game.

6. The man is in a (good, bad) mood.

4 ► **Write a conditional sentence—possible or contrary-to-fact—about each conversation.**

1. **René**   How about going out for coffee later?
    Alicia   O.K. Unless I have too much work to do.
    If Alicia *doesn't have too much work to do, she'll go out for coffee later.*

2. **Jeff**   How would you like to play some racquetball?
    Rich   I would, but I'm out of shape.
    If Rich _____
    _____

3. **Heinz**   I wish I had more money.
    Laurie   Why?
    Heinz   I want to buy a house.
    If Heinz _____
    _____

4. **George**   Could you lend me ten dollars?
    Bruce   I might be able to later. First, Warren has to pay back the ten dollars he owes me.
    If Warren _____
    _____

5 ► **Complete the conversations with advice, using contrary-to-fact conditional sentences.**

1.

I always fall asleep in class.

You go to bed too late.

If you went to bed earlier, you wouldn't always fall asleep in class.

2.

I can't find my other shoe.

You can't find your shoe?
_____
_____
_____

3.

The doctor says I should lose some weight.

Why don't you take up a sport?
_____
_____
_____

Lesson 72

1 ▸ **Choose the sentence that means the same or almost the same. Circle *a* or *b*.**

1. How come you're here so early?
   a. How did you get here so early?
   b. Why are you here so early?

2. He's been working for the same company for 25 years.
   a. He was with the same company for 25 years.
   b. He's been with the same company for 25 years.

3. We'll have to go biking sometime.
   a. We're supposed to go biking sometime.
   b. How about going biking sometime?

4. Give me a call, and we can set up a time.
   a. Give me your phone number, and I'll call you to set up a time.
   b. Call me, and we can set up a time.

5. I'm so stressed out!
   a. I'm under a lot of pressure!
   b. I've spent all my money!

6. I've done my homework.
   a. I've been doing my homework.
   b. I did my homework.

2 ▸ **Answer the questions with your own information.**

1. How will you feel if you get a good grade in your English course? How about a bad grade?

   _____

   _____

2. What will you do if you don't feel well tomorrow morning?

   _____

3. What would you do if you won the lottery?

   _____

4. Imagine you could meet your favorite movie star or singer. What would you say to him/her?

   _____

5. If you could travel anywhere in the world, what three countries would you visit?

   _____

Lesson 73

1 ▶ **Listen to each conversation. Then write *That's right* or *That's wrong*.**

1. The woman isn't home very often. *That's right.*
2. The man doesn't have time to go to the dry cleaner's. _____
3. The woman has a lot of money. _____
4. Both men have been working out regularly at the gym. _____
5. Both women have been very busy lately. _____
6. There's nothing good on TV tonight. _____
7. The weather is nice. _____
8. The man would like to be married. _____

2 ▶ **Listen to each conversation and choose the picture that matches. Circle *a* or *b*.**

1.

a.   b.

2.

a.   b.

3 ▶ **In informal speech, the auxiliary verb *have*—as in "What have you been doing lately?"—is often pronounced /əv/ instead of /hæv/. Listen to the sentences and decide which pronunciation you hear: /əv/ or /hæv/. Check (✔) the correct column.**

	/əv/	/hæv/
1.	___	✔
2.	___	___
3.	___	___
4.	___	___
5.	___	___
6.	___	___
7.	___	___
8.	___	___

Lesson 74

► **Read this letter and then write a reply. Be sure to answer the questions asked in the letter, using your own information.**

> December 4
>
> Dear _____,
>
>   I haven't written any letters in ages because I've been so busy, but I've been thinking about you lately. I just got a scholarship to study in the U.S., and I'll probably go there in September. I'm not sure where I want to go yet, but I want to find a college with a good English program.
>
>   I've been studying very hard, so I haven't had much free time. I've been swimming of course, and I've seen a few movies—but that's about all.
>
>   How have you been? What have you been doing lately? Have you been anywhere exciting? Please write soon.
>
>   Love,
>   Carmen

Review of units 8-11

1 ▶ Complete the conversation with *if* or *unless*.

Wayne   Dad, _____*if*_____ you have time, could you help me with my model airplane?

Mr. Wang   Sure, _____ you want me to.

Wayne   I do, _____ you're too busy.

Mr. Wang   I have some time. Now, you should never build a model _____ you've read the instructions. Have you read them?

Wayne   Yes, and I was thinking about what you're always telling me.

Mr. Wang   What's that?

Wayne   "_____ a job is worth doing, it's worth doing right."

2 ▶ Complete the conversation with reflexive pronouns.

Mr. Wang   Can you figure out that part by _____*yourself*_____, Wayne?

Wayne   I think so. Let me try to do it by _____.

Mrs. Wang   Are you two enjoying _____?

Mr. Wang   How about it, Wayne? Are we enjoying _____?

Wayne   You bet.

Mr. Wang   Wayne has done almost all of it by _____. Most of the time, I just sit here and watch.

Wayne   Do you want to help, Mom?

Mr. Wang   I think your mom needs some time to _____.

Mrs. Wang   Yes, I've got some things to do. Besides, you're doing just fine. Remember to leave _____ enough time to clean up before bed, though.

3 ▶ Complete the conversation with affirmative or negative forms of *be supposed to* or *have to*.

Mr. Wang   Now, what _____*are*_____ we _____*supposed to*_____ do next?

Wayne   Let's see. The instructions say to put together the left wing. You _____ help me anymore, though.

Mr. Wang   You _____ fire your helper, Wayne! Besides, I'm having a great time. Just tell me what you want me to do.

Wayne   Well, first, you _____ put your elbow on the tail. Now I _____ do it all over again.

Mr. Wang   Oh, I'm sorry. I'll try to be more careful.
    (*Later*)

Wayne   Well, that was fun. We _____ pick it up yet, though. It's not dry.

Mr. Wang   It will be dry soon. It _____ take only ten minutes.

4 ▶ **Complete the conversation with the present perfect or present perfect continuous form of the verbs in parentheses. Use affirmative or negative forms.**

Todd Aida, _____*have*_____ you _____*seen*_____ (see) Jeff Madison? I really need to talk to him.

Aida No, but I _____ (be) at my desk. I _____ (work) in the supply room. _____ you _____ (look) in Mr. Perry's office? I know Jeff _____ (work) with him on some special project.

Todd No, but I think I _____ (look) everywhere else. ... Oh, there he is! Jeff! I _____ (look for) you!

Jeff I _____ (be) in Mr. Perry's office.

5 ▶ **Here is some advice that Dr. Berger gave his patients. Rewrite the advice, using *If I were you* ... .**

1. You shouldn't worry so much.
   If I were you, I wouldn't worry so much.

2. You should take better care of yourself.
   _____

3. You'd better not do so much.
   _____

4. You ought to eat less and exercise more.
   _____

6 ▶ **Dr. Berger is always polite to his patients, but when he talks to his nurse, he's more direct. Rewrite what he said to her about his patients, using statements beginning with *If* ... .**

1. Mr. Beasley feels sick because he worries so much.
   If Mr. Beasley didn't worry so much, he wouldn't feel sick.

2. Mrs. Watson is sick because she doesn't take care of herself.
   _____

3. Ms. Garcia gets so exhausted because she does so much.
   _____

4. Mr. Bigelow doesn't lose weight because he eats so much and doesn't exercise more.
   _____

Lesson 75

▶ **Read each conversation. Then complete the summary.**

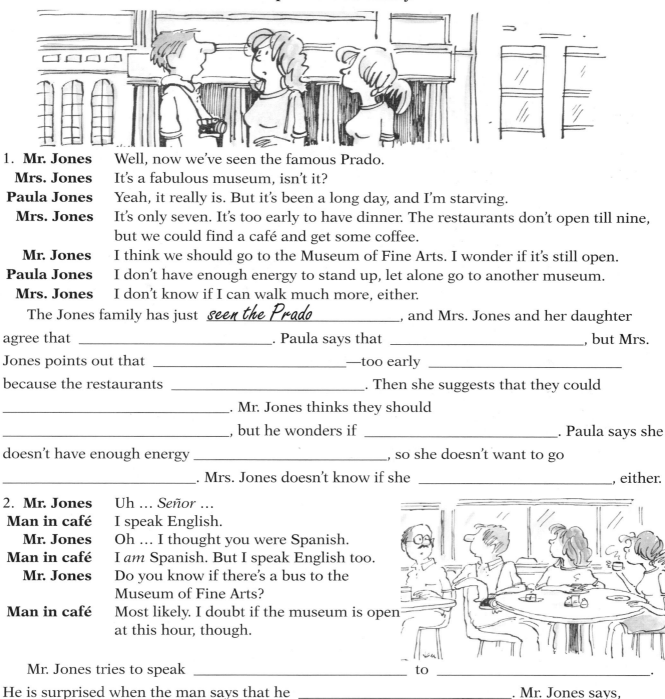

1. **Mr. Jones**   Well, now we've seen the famous Prado.
   Mrs. Jones   It's a fabulous museum, isn't it?
   Paula Jones   Yeah, it really is. But it's been a long day, and I'm starving.
   Mrs. Jones   It's only seven. It's too early to have dinner. The restaurants don't open till nine,
                     but we could find a café and get some coffee.
   Mr. Jones   I think we should go to the Museum of Fine Arts. I wonder if it's still open.
   Paula Jones   I don't have enough energy to stand up, let alone go to another museum.
   Mrs. Jones   I don't know if I can walk much more, either.

The Jones family has just *seen the Prado*_____, and Mrs. Jones and her daughter

agree that _____. Paula says that _____, but Mrs.

Jones points out that _____—too early _____

because the restaurants _____. Then she suggests that they could

_____. Mr. Jones thinks they should

_____, but he wonders if _____. Paula says she

doesn't have enough energy _____, so she doesn't want to go

_____. Mrs. Jones doesn't know if she _____, either.

2. **Mr. Jones**   Uh … *Señor* …
   Man in café   I speak English.
   Mr. Jones   Oh … I thought you were Spanish.
   Man in café   I *am* Spanish. But I speak English too.
   Mr. Jones   Do you know if there's a bus to the
                      Museum of Fine Arts?
   Man in café   Most likely. I doubt if the museum is open
                      at this hour, though.

Mr. Jones tries to speak _____ to _____.

He is surprised when the man says that he _____. Mr. Jones says,

"_____." The man answers, "_____.

But _____." When Mr. Jones asks the man if he knows if there's

_____, the man says, "_____." He goes on to

say that he doubts if _____, though.

Lesson 76

1 ▶ **Find the three conversations.**

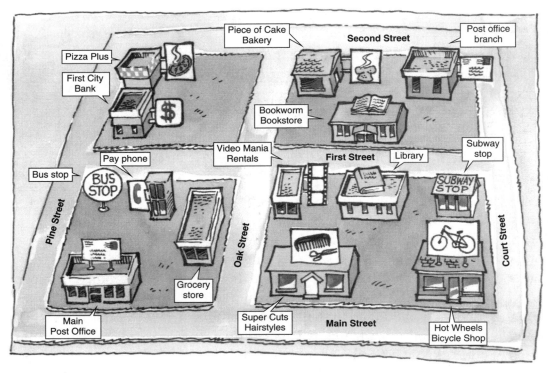

_1_ **A** Do you know if there's a hairstyling salon around here?

_2_ **A** Could you tell me if there's a bicycle shop around here?

_3_ **A** Do you know if there's a post office around here?

____ **B** There's one on the corner of Main and Pine.

____ **B** There's one on the corner of Main and Court.

____ **B** There's one on the corner of Main and Oak.

____ **A** I wonder if you need an appointment.

____ **A** I wonder if it's open late.

____ **A** I wonder if they do repairs.

____ **B** I doubt if they do.

____ **B** I'm not sure if it is.

____ **B** I don't know if you do.

2 ▶ **Listen to each conversation. Then complete the sentences.**

1. She wants to know if _there's a bank in the neighborhood_ _____.

2. They wonder if _____.

3. He isn't sure if _____.

4. She's asking if _____.

5. He'd like to know if _____.

6. They want to know if _____.

3 ▶ **Toshi is thinking about taking his first trip to Chicago this weekend. He's talking to his roommate, Louis. Complete the conversation.**

Toshi   You've been to Chicago, haven't you, Louis?

Louis   Sure. Several times.

Toshi   Do you know if *there are any good hotels near the Loop?*

Louis   Good hotels near the Loop? Let me think. There's the Century. That's pretty nice.

Toshi   Do you know if _____

Louis   All hotels in big cities are expensive. A room at a hotel will cost you at least $75.00.

Toshi   I'm not sure if _____

That's a lot of money.

Louis   How about the YMCA? It would be cheaper, and there's one right near the Loop.

Toshi   I wonder if _____

Louis   I don't know. It's the busy season, so they might be full. Why don't you call and check?

Toshi   I think I will. Do you know if _____

Louis   I doubt if their number is in our phone book. I think you'll have to call the Chicago information number to get it.

4 ▶ **Toshi calls the YMCA in Chicago. Complete the conversation, using expressions such as *Could you tell me if … ?* and *Do you know if … ?***

YMCA
(Lawson Branch)
30 W. Chicago Ave.
Chicago, IL 60610

- 1,200 rooms, 700 with private bath
- TV available at additional charge
- complete gymnasium facilities
- swimming pool on the roof terrace
- cafeteria open 24 hours a day,
  7 days a week

Clerk   YMCA.

Toshi   Hello. *Could you tell me if you have a single room available for Friday night?*

Clerk   A single room for Friday night? … Yes, we do. That's $35.00 a night, with private bath.

Toshi   _____

Clerk   A TV? You can have one put in your room for an additional charge.

Toshi   _____

Clerk   Oh, yes. There are a lot of restaurants in the area, and we have a cafeteria right here in the building.

Toshi   _____

Clerk   Yes, we have a pool on the roof terrace. We have complete gym facilities too.

Toshi   _____

Clerk   No, we can't cash them here, sir. You'd have to take your traveler's checks to a bank.

Toshi   Well, I'd like to make a reservation.

Lesson 77

1 ▶ **Complete the conversations, using emphatic forms.**

1. **A** I thought you were from Brazil.
   B *I am from Brazil* _____, but my parents live in Mexico now.
2. **A** I thought you were French.
   B _____, but I lived in Italy for many years.
3. **A** I thought history was your favorite subject.
   B _____, but I also like math.
4. **A** I thought you liked pizza.
   B _____. I just don't want any right now.
5. **A** I thought you were doing your homework.
   B _____. My teacher told us to watch this TV program.

2 ▶ **Read Sam's letter to his parents. Then complete Sam's conversation with his friend Mel.**

> Dear Mom and Dad,
>   Just a quick note to tell you about my plans. I'm leaving
> for Hawaii on June 17. (I'm going by myself.) The trip takes about
> five hours by plane from San Francisco. I'm going to stay at the
> Reef Hotel in Honolulu, which is on the island of Oahu. If I like
> it there, I may stay for two weeks. I may even look for work while
> I'm there. As you know, I'm really unhappy at my present job and
> have been thinking of quitting.
>   I'll send you a postcard from Hawaii.
>   Love,
>   Sam

Mel When are you leaving, the tenth?
Sam *No, the seventeenth.* _____
Mel You're going alone, aren't you?
Sam _____
Mel How long does the trip take, about eight hours?
Sam _____
Mel Honolulu is on the island of Maui, isn't it?
Sam _____
Mel How long are you going to stay there?
Sam _____

I may even look for work while I'm there. I think I can find a job fixing cars.

3 ▶ **Complete the statements, using the information in exercise 2.**

1. Mel thought *Sam was leaving* _____ on the tenth.
2. Mel knew _____ alone.
3. Mel didn't know _____ five hours.
4. Mel thought _____ on the island of Maui.
5. Sam thought _____ there. He thought _____ a job fixing cars.

Lesson 78

1 ▶ **Describe your favorite dish. Follow the example.**

My favorite dish is paella. Paella is Spanish, and it's a rice dish made with seafood, chicken, and spices. It's cooked slowly in a large pan.

_____

_____

_____

_____

2 ▶ **Complete the conversations with objections, using *too ... to* and the adjectives in parentheses.**

1. **A** Let's go jogging.
   B Now? *I'm too tired to go jogging.* _____ (tired)

2. **A** Do you want to go swimming?
   B Are you kidding? _____ (cold)

3. **A** Are you ready for lunch?
   B Are you serious? _____ (early)

3 ▶ **Complete the conversations with objections, using *not ... enough ... to* and a noun.**

1. **A** Do you want to see the exhibit?
   B *I don't have enough money to see the exhibit.* _____

2. **A** Let's make a chocolate cake.
   B _____

3. **A** How would you like to go to a movie?
   B _____

Lesson 79

1 ▶ **Look at the names of the foods in the box and decide what kind of food they are. Write each word in the correct column. (Some words can go into more than one column.)**

apples	cereal	juice	oysters	pork	shrimp
beef	cheese	lamb	pasta	potato chips	soda
bread	coconut	lobster	peas	potatoes	spinach
cake	fish	milk	peppers	rice	tomatoes
candy	grapes	mineral water	pie	scallops	yogurt

Meat	Seafood	Vegetables	Fruit	Dairy	Grains	Dessert/Snacks	Drinks

2 ▶ **Answer the questions with your own information.**

1. What are three foods you usually eat raw (without cooking them)?

_____

2. What five foods do you like cooked in the oven?

_____

3. What do you like to eat when the weather is very hot? And when it's very cold?

_____

  3 ▶ **Listen to each conversation. Circle *Yes* if the picture is correct. Circle *No* if it is not correct.**

1.
Yes
No

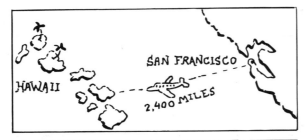

2.
Yes
No

3.
Yes
No

4.
Yes
No

Lesson 80

1 ▶ **Listen and complete each conversation. Circle *a*, *b*, or *c*.**

1. a. I doubt if there is.
   b. Sorry, I can't think of one.
   c. Most likely.

2. a. Yes, you can.
   b. I'd like some information.
   c. I'm sure you can.

3. a. It is.
   b. It was.
   c. I do.

4. a. I doubt if it is.
   b. I'm not sure if they are.
   c. I don't know if it does.

5. a. I'm too angry to talk.
   b. I'm too tired to walk.
   c. We don't have enough time to walk.

6. a. I think he may know what to do.
   b. I didn't think he would know what to do.
   c. I was sure he'd know what to do.

2 ▶ **Listen to the conversations and mark the strongest vowel or vowel combination in each sentence.**

1. **A** I thought you taught Portuguese.
   B I do teach Portuguese.
2. **A** I thought you were Argentinian.
   B No, I'm Uruguayan.
3. **A** Let's go to a museum.
   B I'm too tired to go to a museum.
4. **A** Let's go out for dinner tonight.
   B We don't have enough money to go out for dinner.

Lesson 81

▶ **Read the review of Claude's Kitchen. Then write a review of your favorite restaurant for a local newspaper. Write about the last meal you had there.**

EATING OUT

CLAUDE'S KITCHEN

by Raoul Stendall

Claude's Kitchen isn't very large, but the food is good. Claude Didier does the cooking, and his menu includes a lot of New Orleans French, or Cajun, favorites. While I was there I had gumbo. This tasty mixture of ham and fish is cooked in a heavy pot. I thought it was delicious. For dessert, I had apple surprise, a mixture of cooked apples and dough. It was too sweet for me, but you might like it if you have a sweet tooth. Claude has different kinds of coffee, and my espresso was a perfect end to a good dinner.

Claude's Kitchen, located at 311 Bourbon Street, is open for dinner every evening until 11:00, Tuesday through Sunday. The restaurant gets very busy, so be sure to make a reservation before you go.

_____

by_____

_____

_____

_____

_____

_____

_____

_____

_____

Lesson 82

▶ **Put the lines of the conversation in order. Then write the conversation.**

_____ May I help you?

_____ Well, these sweaters are lovely.

_1_ I really appreciate your coming with me, Alex. I have so much trouble picking out gifts.

_____ This one?

_____ Hmm … Could I see that striped one on the bottom shelf?

_____ I'm trying to buy a gift for a friend, but I'm not sure what to get her.

_____ You have good taste, sir. This is a beauty.

_____ Uh, no, I don't. I guess I should have found out.

_____ Well, take your time. Look around, and maybe you'll get inspired.

_____ It's nice, Alex.

_____ I don't know. What if Andrea doesn't like stripes?

_____ Do you know what size your friend wears?

_____ Oh, I'm sure she'll like it.

_____ No, the one with the blue stripes.

A _I really appreciate your coming with me, Alex. I have so much trouble picking out gifts._

B _____

_____

C _____

A _____

_____

C _____

A _____

C _____

A _____

C _____

B _____

A _____

B _____

C _____

A _____

Lesson 83

1 ► Write phrases describing the clothes in the pictures. (Use your imagination to say what material each thing is made of.)

1. *a plaid shirt made of cotton*

1.

2. _____

2.

3. _____

3.

4. _____

4.

5. _____

5.

6. _____

6.

2 ► Complete the conversations between the shoppers and the salesclerks.

1. **A** Could I see that tie, please?
   B *Which one?* _____
   A The striped one.
   B It's a nice tie. Is it for you or a gift?
   A _____ I'm going to give it to him for Father's Day.

2. **A** _____
   B Which shoes?
   A The black ones. _____
   B They're 100 percent leather. Would you like to try them on?
   A No, thank you. These heels are a little too high. _____
   _____
   B Yes. I can show you the same shoe with a low heel.

3. **A** _____
   B The one with long sleeves?
   A _____ I never wear shirts with long sleeves during the summer.
   B Here you are. It's a very nice shirt.
   A _____
   B It's 100 percent cotton.

3 ▶ **Complete the conversation.**

A I want to buy something for my nephew, but *I'm not sure what to get him.*

B Do you know if he has any hobbies?

A Yes, as a matter of fact, _____

B Oh, then why don't you get him a stamp album?

A That's a good idea. Oh, and I don't know what to get my niece either.

B _____

A I know she likes music.

B _____

A No, unfortunately, I don't have the slightest idea what kind of music she likes.

4 ▶ **Combine the expressions and the questions in the box to form embedded questions. Then complete the conversation with the embedded questions.**

Do you remember … ? Do they come in king size too?
Would you tell me … ? How much did it cost?
Does it say … ? Do they have any other styles?
Do you have any idea … ? What's it made of?
Do you remember … ? Where did you get it?
Do you know … ? Is it washable?

A What a nice blanket! *Do you remember where you got it?* _____

B I ordered it from a catalogue.

A _____

B Sure, it's no secret. It was $25.95.

A _____

B Oh, yes. It doesn't have to be dry-cleaned.

A _____

B I think it's 100 percent cotton.

A You have a queen-size bed, don't you? _____

_____

B Most likely. Let me check the catalogue. I still have it. … Yes. The king size is $30.95.

A I'm not sure I want plaid, though. _____

_____

B Yes. It comes in solid colors too.

Lesson 84

1 ▶ **Complete the conversations with the sentences in the box.**

> What if my husband doesn't like them?
> Don't worry. It won't.
> What if they cut it too short?
> What if it rains?
> Oh, I'm sure he will.
> I think she will.
> What if our candidate doesn't win?
> Oh, I'm sure they won't.

1. **A** I just bought these curtains for the living room.
   What if my husband doesn't like them?

   B _____

2. **A** I'm planning to go camping this weekend.

   _____

   B _____

3. **A** I've decided to get my hair cut.

   _____

   B _____

4. **A** The election is tomorrow.

   _____

   B _____

2 ▶ **Change the second sentence to a question that expresses a concern.**

1. I just bought a sweater without trying it on. I'm afraid it won't fit.
   What if it doesn't fit?

2. Jason said he'd lend me some money. I'm afraid he'll change his mind.

   _____

3. Rebecca's choosing a college. I'm worried that she'll make the wrong decision.

   _____

4. We've made the first payment on our new car. I'm afraid we won't have enough money for the rest of the payments.

   _____

Lesson 85

1 ▶ Complete the conversations, using *should have* or *shouldn't have* and the correct form of the verb in parentheses.

1. **A** I really like the shirt, but it's too small.
   B I thought your arms were shorter. *I should have bought a bigger size.* (buy)

2. **A** Is that your new tie? It has a stain on it.
   B You're kidding! I guess _____ (look over)

3. **A** Gail only likes classical music.
   B Oh, no! I just got her a country-music CD. _____
   _____ (get)

4. **A** Sarah isn't supposed to eat candy.
   B _____ (give)

5. **A** Your new sweater looks a little too small for you.
   B I know. _____ (try on)

2 ▶ Make two judgments about each situation—one with *should have* and one with *shouldn't have*. Follow the example.

1. a. *He should have worn warmer clothes.*
   _____

   b. *He shouldn't have worn shorts and a t-shirt.*
   _____

2. a. _____
   _____

   b. _____
   _____

3. a. _____
   _____

   b. _____
   _____

4. a. _____
   _____

   b. _____
   _____

Lesson 86

1 ▶ Complete the conversation, using the information in the box.

> What size does she wear?
> Does Mom wear wool sweaters?
> What should we get them?
> Do Mom and Dad still like Frank Sinatra?
> What kind of perfume does she use?
> Is he still interested in photography?
> What are they made of?

A I really don't know what Mom and Dad want for their anniversary. Do you have any idea
what we should get them?

B Yeah, I have some ideas. I was thinking of getting Mom perfume. Do you remember

_____

A I think it's called Poison … or something like that. I think I'll get her a sweater. Do you
remember _____

B I think she's a small. Look, there are some sweaters over here. Does it say

_____

A Yes. Wool. Do you know _____

B I think she does. How about Dad? Do you know _____

_____

A No, I don't think so. He gave that up last year. Oh, I have an idea! Why don't we get them a
few CDs? Do you remember _____

B They love him. Listen, that's a great idea. Let's go find the music department.

2 ▶ Read the situations and decide what you would say to the people.

1. You think a friend made a mistake when she bought a very large computer.

_____

2. You think your teacher gave you too much homework last week.

_____

3. You were rude to a coworker, and you regret it.

_____

4. A friend has applied for a job, but he doesn't know yet if he got it. You're worried because he
went out and bought an expensive new car.

_____

5. You ask one friend if she knows if another friend has any hobbies.

_____

Lesson 87

1 ▶ **Listen to each conversation. Then circle the correct statement.**

1. a. He knows Helga very well.
   b. He hasn't known Helga for very long.

2. a. They should have bought a bigger car.
   b. They shouldn't have bought such an expensive car.

3. a. She should have called first.
   b. She shouldn't have come so late.

4. a. She's worried that Harvey won't like the pants.
   b. She's sorry that Harvey doesn't like the pants.

5. a. He's buying a striped shirt in size large.
   b. He's buying a plaid shirt in size medium.

6. a. She should have brought her book to class.
   b. She shouldn't have brought her book to class.

2 ▶ **Listen to the sentences and check (✔) the words you hear.**

	should	*shouldn't*	*should have*	*shouldn't have*
1.	_____	_____	_____	___✔___
2.	_____	_____	_____	_____
3.	_____	_____	_____	_____
4.	_____	_____	_____	_____
5.	_____	_____	_____	_____
6.	_____	_____	_____	_____
7.	_____	_____	_____	_____
8.	_____	_____	_____	_____
9.	_____	_____	_____	_____
10.	_____	_____	_____	_____

3 ▶ **Listen to the questions and mark the intonation. Circle the arrow on the left (↗) when the speaker's voice goes up. Circle the arrow on the right (↘) when the speaker's voice goes down.**

1. ↗ ↘   4. ↗ ↘

2. ↗ ↘   5. ↗ ↘

3. ↗ ↘   6. ↗ ↘

Lesson 88

▶ You have just read the ad from the International English Language Center and are interested in taking some classes there. Write a letter to the director asking for more information. You may use the questions in the box. Begin some of your sentences with *Could you please tell me … ?* and *I'd also like to know … .*

How much is the tuition?
How many hours are in each program?
What is the average class size?
Does the Center have a job adviser?
Is the Center open on Saturdays?
What kind of visa is needed?

Is your English holding you back?

Improve your English at the International English Language Center. Our teachers are trained to teach English to speakers of other languages, and our program has the newest computers to help you learn. Day and evening classes are available. For more information, contact:

**Mr. Peter Cowden
The International Language Center
8 Burlington Gardens
Chiswick, London W5
England**

Lesson 89

▶ **Complete the conversations with the sentences in the box.**

Yes. He said he'd be here at two o'clock sharp.
I didn't have to give him directions. He said he knew where the place was.
    He must not have written down the time.
He had an appointment to go to. He had to be there at three thirty, remember?
I'm sure there's a logical explanation. Something must have come up.
I know. Stop pacing like that. You're making me nervous.
There you are! It's ten to three. What happened?
O.K. I'll stay here and wait for him.
I wonder what's keeping Sam. He was supposed to be here at two.

1. **A** *I wonder what's keeping Sam. He was supposed to be here at two.*

   B Did you tell him I had to be back by three thirty?

   A _____

   B It's already two thirty.

   A _____

   B Do you think he might have gotten lost? He may not have understood your directions.

   A _____
   _____

   B It just isn't like him to be late, though.

   A _____

   B Well, it makes no sense for me to wait any longer. I think I'll just grab a bite to eat and get back.

   A _____

2. **A** _____
   B Hi! I'm sorry I'm late. The bus broke down. I couldn't get another one or a taxi, so I had to walk. Where's George?

   A _____

   B Oh, I'm really sorry. I'll have to apologize to George when I see him.

Lesson 90

1 ► **Complete the conversations using** *may (not) have* **or** *might (not) have* **and the correct form of the verb in parentheses.**

1. **A** I wonder why Sam's Grocery Store is closed. It's always open—24 hours a day, 7 days a week.

   B There *may have been* _____ (be) a fire, or someone _____ (break into) the store.

   A I doubt that. Sam _____ (go) on vacation. Or he _____ (decide) to close the store for a change. After all, it is Independence Day.

2. **A** I tried to call Ingrid last night, but she didn't answer.

   B She _____ (go) out.

   A I don't think so. She never goes out during the week.

   B Well, she _____ (turn) the phone off.

   A Why would she do that?

   B She _____ (sleep), and she _____ (want) to be disturbed.

2 ► **Write conclusions with** *must (not)*, **using the ideas in the pictures.**

Bart

The Wilsons' house

1. *Bart must have broken his leg while he was skiing.* _____

2. _____

Celia

Claude and Helen

3. _____

4. _____

3 ▸ Change the underlined sentences to affirmative or negative sentences with *may have*, *might have*, or *must have*.

1. **A** Hello? Hello? … Someone hung up.
   B It stopped ringing before you got here. I wonder who it was.
   A <u>Maybe it was Dean.</u> I've been waiting for his call.
   It might have been Dean.

2. **A** Where is that recipe for chicken teriyaki?
   B Can't you find it?
   A No. <u>I probably lent it to someone who didn't give it back.</u>
   _____

3. **A** I don't think I turned off the oven before we left the house. Did you?
   B No, I didn't. <u>Maybe I didn't turn off the lights, either.</u> We'd better go back.
   _____

4. **A** Why don't you ask Carol to go to the movie with us?
   B <u>I'd like to, but maybe she's seen it already.</u>
   _____

5. **A** Have you heard from Jessica?
   B No, I haven't. <u>She probably didn't want to go with us.</u>
   _____

6. **A** Look! The door is open and the lock is broken.
   B <u>The office was probably broken into during the night.</u>
   _____

7. **A** I saw Joe downtown today, and he was driving a beautiful new car.
   B <u>Maybe it was his mother's.</u> She just bought a new car.
   _____

8. **A** Are those shoes the right size? They look too big for you.
   B <u>I asked for a size 8, but the salesperson probably gave me a 9.</u>
   _____

4 ▸ Listen to each conversation and decide if someone is stating a possibility or stating a conclusion. Check (✔) the correct column.

	Stating a possibility	Stating a conclusion
1.	✔	_____
2.	_____	_____
3.	_____	_____
4.	_____	_____
5.	_____	_____
6.	_____	_____

Lesson 91

1 ▶ The people in the pictures were all late for appointments today. What excuse do you think each person gave? Write an excuse for each person, using *so* and *had to*.

1. *I'm sorry I'm late. My wallet was stolen, so I had to go to the police station.*

2. _____

3. _____

4. _____

2 ▶ Complete the conversations with past forms of *be supposed to* or *have to*.

1. **A** Isn't John here yet?
   B No, he isn't, and he ___*was supposed to*___ be here half an hour ago.

2. **A** Did Marcia leave?
   B She couldn't stay. She _____ catch the last bus.

3. **A** I'm looking for Mr. Kent. I _____ meet him here at 2:00.
   B Are you Mr. Fleming? He asked me to tell you he'll be a little late. He
   _____ go to a meeting, but he should be back in a few minutes.

4. **A** I wonder where Grace and Julio are. They _____ get here by 8:15.
   B Oh, they just called. Their baby-sitter _____ be there at 8:00, but he
   _____ cancel. If they can find another sitter, they'll be here soon.

Lesson 92

1 ▶ **Report each conversation by changing direct speech to reported speech.**

1. **Vince** I'm sorry I can't stay, Joan. I have to get home. My children are home all by themselves.

   Joan I don't want to make you late, Vince. I'll talk to you soon.

   a. Vince told Joan _(that) he was sorry he couldn't stay._

   b. He said _____

   c. He said _____

   d. Joan said _____

   e. She told him _____

2. **Gary** The phone is ringing, and the call may be for me. I don't want to interrupt the meeting, though.

   Ana That's all right, Gary. We need a break. We'll meet again in five minutes.

   a. Gary said _____

   _____

   b. He said _____

   c. Ana told him _____

   d. She said _____

   e. She said _____

2 ▶ **Listen to each sentence in direct speech and choose the sentence that matches it in reported speech.**

_c_	1.	a. She said she'd try to come to the party.
___	2.	b. He told us that he couldn't make it any earlier.
___	3.	c. He said he was taking care of his little sister Thursday night.
___	4.	d. She told them she didn't have enough money for her rent.
___	5.	e. He told them that he was in love.
___	6.	f. She told them she wanted them to meet her new boyfriend.
___	7.	g. She said she wouldn't be able to get to work on time.
___	8.	h. He told them that their English was improving.
___	9.	i. She said she wasn't going to be able to take a vacation next month.
___	10.	j. He said he had an appointment at four o'clock.
___	11.	k. She told him she couldn't stay very long.
___	12.	l. She said she wasn't planning to go to the party.

Lesson 93

1 ▶ Follow the conversation and mark the box next to the sentences you hear.

Father ■ We really need to speak to Debbie's teacher.
Father ☐ We really should speak to Debbie's teacher.

Mother ☐ Why? Debbie's doing very well in school.
Mother ☐ How come? Debbie's very happy in school.

Father ☐ I'm worried about her math. She still doesn't know very much.
Father ☐ I'm worried about her math. She still can't do very much.

Mother ☐ Bob, Debbie's only four years old! She'll learn to add and subtract in first grade.
Mother ☐ Bob, Debbie's only five years old! She'll learn to add and subtract next year.

Father ☐ I guess you're right. There's no reason to worry.
Father ☐ I guess you're right. There's nothing to worry about.

2 ▶ Look at the sentences you marked in exercise 1 and report the conversation, using *said* or *told* in your answers.

He told her (that) they really needed to speak to Debbie's teacher.

_____

_____

_____

_____

_____

_____

_____

3 ▶ Write three sentences about things you were supposed to do over the past few days but didn't do because you had to do something else. Follow the example.

I was supposed to cook dinner last night, but I had to work late.

1. _____

2. _____

3. _____

Lesson 94

 1 ► **Listen and choose the sentence that means the same or almost the same as the sentence you hear. Circle *a* or *b*.**

1. a. He doesn't like to be late.
   b. He's usually on time.

2. a. Maybe he didn't understand my directions.
   b. He probably didn't understand my directions.

3. a. He picked her up at 6:30.
   b. He'll pick her up at 6:30.

4. a. I thought you wanted to go out tonight.
   b. I thought you wanted to stay home tonight.

5. a. She was supposed to walk, but she took the bus instead.
   b. She was supposed to take the bus, but she walked instead.

6. a. Maybe his secretary forgot to tell him about the appointment.
   b. His secretary probably forgot to tell him about the appointment.

2 ► **Peggy Barnes is still working hard at her restaurant, and her parents are worried. Listen to each part of their conversation. Then choose *a* or *b*.**

Part 1

1. a. Peggy and her mother were supposed to go shopping today.
   b. Peggy had to cancel her plans with her mother.

Part 2

2. a. Peggy told her mother that she would call her back.
   b. Peggy asked her mother to call her back.

3. a. Peggy was supposed to do some last-minute shopping.
   b. Peggy had to do some last-minute shopping.

4. a. Peggy might have called while her mother was out.
   b. Peggy must not have called back.

Part 3

5. a. Peggy must have gotten someone to wash the dishes.
   b. Peggy was supposed to get somebody to wash the dishes.

3 ► **Peggy's parents have a conversation later the same evening. Listen and choose the correct pictures.**

1. a.   b.   2. a.   b.

Lesson 95

▶ You recently moved to a new city, and you just got this letter from your friend Mark. Mark is very worried about Ken, another good friend of yours. Read the letter and then answer it. You may use the expressions in the box.

| He might have … |
| He must have … |
| He may not have … |
| He was supposed to … |
| He told me that … |

Dear _____,

June 20, _____

I'm writing to you because I'm a little worried about Ken. I've been calling his apartment all week and nobody answers the phone.

Ken didn't say anything to me about taking a trip. I know you and he were really good friends all last year, so I thought maybe he told you something about his plans. I'd appreciate it if you'd write me a note if you know anything about this. I've thought about going to the police, but he may just be on vacation.

I hope you're doing well.

Regards,
Mark

_____
_____,

_____
_____
_____
_____
_____
_____

_____,
_____

Review of units 12–14

1 ▶ In *a*, change the direct speech to reported speech. In *b*, write two sentences using *may have, might have, must have,* or *should have.* Make one sentence affirmative and one negative.

1. **a.**   **b.**

a. The directions said *to bake the cake for 45 minutes.*

b. Tom and Cindy *must have baked the cake too long. They must not have followed the directions.*

2. **a.**   **b.**

a. Mr. Boden said _____

_____

He said _____

_____

b. Mr. Boden _____

_____

_____

3. **a.**   **b.**

a. Aunt Graciela said _____

_____

_____

b. Aunt Graciela _____

_____

_____

4. **a.**   **b.**

a. Katherine said _____

_____

She said _____

_____

b. Katherine _____

_____

_____

2 ▶ Pierre Leconte is the receptionist at a small hotel in Honolulu, Hawaii. These are some of the things hotel guests want to know. Rewrite their questions, beginning them with *Could you tell me ... ?*, *Do you know ... ?*, or *Do you have any idea ... ?*

1. Where's Kalakaua Boulevard?
   Could you tell me where Kalakaua Boulevard is?

2. Is the Ala Moana Post Office near here?
   _____

3. What time does the show at the Kahala Hilton start?
   _____

4. Is the Honolulu Symphony Orchestra playing tonight?
   _____

5. How much will a good dinner at The Third Floor cost?
   _____

6. Are there any Korean restaurants nearby?
   _____

3 ▶ Pierre overheard some guests' conversation. Complete the conversation with objections, using *too ... to* and *not ... enough ... to*.

A Let's go jogging on the beach.
B *I'm too tired to go jogging on the beach.*
A Oh, I didn't know you were tired. Well, let's go out for lunch.
B _____
A You're right. We just had breakfast a few hours ago. O.K., how about going swimming in the pool?
B _____
A Not warm enough? The temperature is above 80. I know! Let's go shopping.
B _____
A Well, *I* have enough money. I'll lend you some.

4 ▶ Think of a famous person that you know something about. Write at least four sentences about his or her life. Follow the example.

Steffi Graf must have learned to play tennis when she was very young. She might not have finished high school because she started playing professional tennis when she was a teenager. She really should have stayed in school a little longer. I wonder if she's happy, and I wonder what she'll do when she stops playing tennis.

_____
_____
_____
_____
_____